The Sources of Roman L

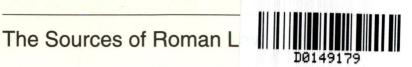

D0149179

The notion and understanding of law penetrated society in Ancient Rome to a degree unparalleled in modern times. The poet Juvenal, for instance, described the virtuous man as a good soldier, faithful guardian, incorruptible judge and honest witness.

This book is concerned with four central questions: Who made law? Where did a Roman go to discover what the law was? How has the law survived to be known to us today? And what procedures were there for putting the law into effect? In *The Sources of Roman Law*, the origins of law and their relative weight are described in the light of developing Roman history. This is a topic that appeals to a wide range of readers. The law student will find illumination for the study of the substantive law. The student of history will be guided into an appreciation of what Roman law means, as well as its value for the understanding and interpretation of Roman history. Both will find invaluable the description of how the sources have survived to inform our legal system and pose their problems for us.

O.F.Robinson, Reader in Law at the University of Glasgow, is a Roman lawyer and legal historian. She has published widely on Roman criminal and administrative law and is the author of *Ancient Rome: City Planning and Administration* (1992) and *The Criminal Law of Ancient Rome* (1995).

Approaching the Ancient World
Series editor: Richard Stoneman

The sources for the study of the Greek and Roman world are diffuse, diverse, and often complex, and special training is needed in order to use them to the best advantage in constructing a historical picture.

The books in this series provide an introduction to the problems and methods involved in the study of ancient history. The topics covered will range from the use of literary sources for Greek history and for Roman history, through numismatics, epigraphy, and dirt archaeology, to the use of legal evidence and of art and artefacts in chronology. There will also be books on statistical and comparative method, and on feminist approaches.

The Uses of Greek Mythology
Ken Dowden

Art, Artefacts, and Chronology in Classical Archaeology
William R. Biers

Reading Papyri, Writing Ancient History
Roger S. Bagnall

Ancient History from Coins
Christopher Howgego

The Sources of Roman Law
Olivia Robinson

The Sources of Roman Law

Problems and Methods for Ancient Historians

O.F. Robinson

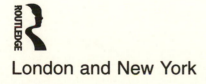

London and New York

First published in 1997
by Routledge
11 New Fetter Lane, London EC4P 4EE

Simultaneously published in the USA and Canada
by Routledge
29 West 35th Street, New York, NY 10001

Typeset in Baskerville by Keystroke, Jacaranda Lodge, Wolverhampton

Printed and bound in Great Britain by TJ Press (Padstow) Ltd,
Padstow, Cornwall

British Library Cataloguing in Publication Data
A catalogue record for this book is available from the British Library

Library of Congress Cataloguing in Publication Data
Robinson, O. F.
    The sources of Roman law : problems and methods for ancient
    historians / O.F. Robinson
    p. cm – (Approaching the ancient world)
    Includes bibliographical references and index.
    1. Roman law–Sources. I. Title. II. Series.
    KJA190.R63 1997
    340.5′4–dc20   96–7551
            CIP

ISBN 0–415–08994–8
      0–415–08995–6 (pbk)

Contents

Preface

This book attempts to explain the nature of the sources of Roman law, and to discuss their use both then and now. The first chapter gives an outline history of Roman law, designed to show the authority of those responsible for the different forms taken by the sources; it also shows the changing balance between them. Then, in the second chapter, the sources are looked at with a lawyer's definition: where does one go to discover what the law is. Here the different forms, and their relationship with each other, are considered. In the third chapter the focus is on the sources as the information on law available to a modern romanist, and the ways in which the sources have survived. The fourth chapter deals with the mechanisms by which the law was put into effect; how was a source made effective, how in practice did the sources blend, or provide room for conflict. Since so much of the development of Roman law was predicated on forms of process, the sources are difficult to understand without some knowledge of procedure. The fifth chapter looks at the problems of the sources, and the hazards of using them for writing history, even legal history, but far more for social or political history. I hope that students of both Roman history and Roman law will find it useful.

The focus of this book is on private law (the *ius civile* of the Middle Ages). This is largely because private law was the chief interest of the most creative makers of law, the jurists, but partly too because the later influence of Roman law has been predominantly in this field. This means that, inevitably, some institutions of the private law are mentioned, and there is, in general, not space to explain them. The reader who needs help should turn to Berger (1953) for a definition, or to one of the elementary treatises on Roman law such as Borkowski (1994), Lee (1956), Nicholas (1962), Thomas (1976), or Watson (1970); Buckland (1963) remains the standard textbook in English. (There is, incidentally, a deliberate bias towards the English language in the sources cited.) The *Oxford Classical Dictionary* gives basic information about the major historical events and figures, including the emperors.

Since this is an introduction to the sources of Roman law, it is concerned with the ancient world, whether that be taken to mean the Twelve Tables of the early Republic or Justinian. It therefore does not investigate the Romano-Germanic laws, which for the purposes of this book are only of interest as the path by which other, truly Roman, sources were transmitted to the modern world. Similarly it does not deal with the eastern history of Justinian's law, Byzantine law.

Dates are all AD, unless otherwise specified. Quotations from the Digest are taken from the Watson translation, with some modifications, those from the Theodosian Code from Pharr's. The remaining translations are mostly my own.

I owe a considerable debt to Professor Dieter Nörr who, whether or not he realizes it, gave me the idea of how I should shape this book, which came to fruition in Mainz when I should have been thinking of other things. I owe an enormous debt to Professor Alan Watson, with whom I by no means always agree, but who has stimulated my thinking all my Roman law life. I am grateful to him, to Professor Michael Rainer, and to Dr Robert Frakes for reading the whole draft, and making valuable suggestions. I make the usual but truthful disclaimer that they are not responsible for my errors and omissions. Professors Michael Hoeflich and Hagith Sawan also made helpful comments while I was spending a very enjoyable and fruitful semester in the University of Kansas.

I also owe a debt to the magisterial work of Leopold Wenger, which still dominates this field (and in whose eponymous Institute I have finished this book – with further thanks to Professor Dieter Nörr and his assistants). Although it is to compare small things with great, like him I found that the difficulty was to strike a balance between the information needed by lawyers and wanted by historians, to make intelligible to historians a source, or rather a group of sources, which have their own internal development. The historian must have some understanding of legal thought if he is to take full advantage of the possibilities, yet it is not easy for a student to learn to think like a jurist. This is why, on reflection, the people without whom I could not have written this book are my students of the last thirty years: *floreant*!

Abbreviations

ANRW	*Aufstieg und Niedergang der römischen Welt*, ed. H.Temporini [with contributions in English as well as other European languages] (Berlin, 1972–)
Apokrimata	*Apokrimata: Decisions of Septimius Severus on Legal Matters*, ed. W.L.Westermann & A.A.Schiller (Columbia University Press, 1954)
ARS	*Ancient Roman Statutes*, ed. A.C.Johnson, P.R.Coleman-Norton & F.C.Bourne (University of Texas, 1961)
Bas.	*Basilica*
c.	*constitutio* (imperial enactment)
CAH	*Cambridge Ancient History* (Cambridge University Press, 1923–56, 2nd/3rd edn 1970–)
CIG	*Corpus Inscriptionum Graecarum* (Berlin, 1828–77)
CIL	*Corpus Inscriptionum Latinarum* (Berlin, 1863–)
CJ	*Codex Justinianus* = Justinian's Code of 534
Coll.	*Collatio legum Mosaicarum et Romanarum*
Collectio	*Collectio librorum iuris anteiustiniani*, ed. P.Krüger, T.Mommsen, & G.Studemund, 3 vols, (Berlin, 1878–1927)
CTh	*Codex Theodosianus* = Theodosian Code
D	Digest (sometimes known as *Pandects*)

ELH	O.F.Robinson, T.D.Fergus & W.M.Gordon, *European Legal History* (Butterworth, 2nd edn 1994)
ET	*Edictum Theodorici*
FIRA	*Fontes Iuris Romani Antejustiniani*, ed. S.Riccobono, J.Baviera & V.Arangio-Ruiz, 3 vols (Florence, 2nd edn 1968)
Frag.Dos.	*Fragmentum Dositheanum*
FV	*Fragmenta Vaticana* = Vatican Fragments
G	Gaius' *Institutes*
Gellius	Aulus Gellius *Noctes Atticae*
HS	*sestertii*
IG	*Inscriptiones Graecae* (Berlin, 1873–)
ILS	*Inscriptiones Latinae Selectae*, ed. H.Dessau (Berlin, 1892–1916)
Index Interpolationum	*Index Interpolationum quae in Iustiniani Digestis inesse dicuntur*, with Supplement, ed. E.Levy & E.Rabel (Weimar, 1929–35)
Inst	*Institutes* or *Institutions* of Justinian
IRMAE	*Ius Romanum Medii Aevi*
Iurisprudentia	*Iurisprudentiae anteiustinianae reliquias in usum maxime academicum compositas quae supersunt a* P.E.Huschke, 6th edn by E.Seckel & B.Kübler (Teubner, Leipzig,1908–27)
Jolowicz	Jolowicz, H.F. & Nicholas, B. *Historical Introduction to the Study of Roman Law* (Cambridge University Press, 3rd edn 1972)
LRB	*Lex Romana Burgundionum*
LRV	*Lex Romana Visigothorum*, ed. G.F. Haenel (Leipzig 1849, repr. 1962)
MGH	*Monumenta Germaniae Historica*
Notitia Dignitatum	*Notitia Dignitatum*, ed. O.Seeck (Berlin, 1876)
Nov	*Novella lex* = Novel (imperial enactment subsequent to Code)
NovJ	Novel of Justinian
P.Oxy.	*The Oxyrhynchus Papyri*, ed. B.P.Grenfell, A.S.Hunt, et al. (Egypt Exploration Society, 1898–)

pr.	*principium* (opening sentence of a Digest fragment or Code *lex*)
PS	*Pauli Sententiae* = Opinions of Paul
P-W	*Pauly-Wissowa: Paulys Realencyclopädie der classischen Altertumswissenschaft* (Stuttgart, 1894–)
RE	*Pauly-Wissowa*
Roman Statutes	*Roman Statutes*, ed. M.H.Crawford (London, BICS Supp. 64, 1995)
SC, SCC	*Senatusconsultum, Senatusconsulta* = resolution(s) of the Senate
SIG	*Sylloge Inscriptionum Graecarum*, ed. W.Dittenberger (Leipzig, 1915–24, repr. 1982)
Textes	*Textes de Droit Romain*, ed. P.F.Girard & F.Senn, 7th edn par un groupe de romanistes (Paris 1967)
UE	*Epitome* of Ulpian
VIR	*Vocabularium Iurisprudentiae Romanae*, ed. O.Gradenwitz & B.Kübler et al. (Berlin, 1894–)
XII T	Twelve Tables

Periodicals are abbreviated according to the conventions of *L'Année Philologique*, with the following exceptions: *RHD* for their *RD, TR* for *TRG, SZ* for *ZRG*. Other abbreviations follow the *Oxford Latin Dictionary* (OLD) or the *Oxford Classical Dictionary* (OCD).

Chapter 1

The Makers of Roman Law

THE BEGINNINGS

Once upon a time, and I use the traditional phrase deliberately, Rome was a small city state governed by kings and closely connected to the Etruscans, a relatively advanced people of central Italy, with wide trading links. Rome was probably founded as a community, that is as a potential city state rather than just the site of a few shepherds' huts, as early as the eighth century BC. The traditional date has long been 753 BC, and archaeological evidence shows that the 'city' was certainly in existence by the early sixth century. The rule of the kings at Rome in this period is confirmed by the surviving sacral offices of *interrex* and *rex sacrorum*.[1] There were laws traditionally ascribed to these kings (*leges regiae*), which seem to have been customary rules dealing with matters on the frontier between law (public and private) and religion.[2] They were probably made into a collection quite late in the Republic to explain points of sacral law; they bear no strong resemblance to the law as it was later developed, or even to the Twelve Tables.[3] On those matters that may be classed as private law, the *leges regiae* deal with aspects of the (extended) family. These aspects comprise the power of life and death of the *paterfamilias*, the marriage relationship, Caesarian operations to try saving the child of a dead mother, mourning periods, the citizenship of formally freed slaves, and relations between patron and client.

According to tradition again, in 509 BC the kings were expelled from Rome, and a republic was established. It is quite clear that the republic was for long a society in flux. The portrait given us by the historians (writing at least 400 years later) is of conflict between patricians and plebeians, known as the struggle of the orders; this distinction may only have hardened after the overthrow of the kings. Various attempts at a lasting constitution seem to have been made, at least in the eyes of those who recorded them much later. We hear of plebeian secessions, military tribunes with consular power as well as consuls, of the institution of a (patrician) censorship. However, a settled, although unwritten, constitution for the Republic, as we know it in reliably attested times, was established by the Licinian Sextian Acts of 367 BC. The Urban Praetor and the curule aediles date from them; they also marked the beginning of the end of the struggle of the orders.

However, the legal history of Rome has some different landmarks from the political history. The foundation of Roman law, the legal attitude of Rome, is generally accepted as being based on the Twelve Tables of the mid-fifth century BC. Livy called them 'the source and origins of all our law'.[4] We have no complete account of them, although Cicero indeed says that, as a boy, he had to learn them by heart.[5] What we have instead, is quotations, modernized or paraphrased, from the Twelve Tables, by, among others, Cicero, Festus, and Aulus Gellius to illustrate points they were making. Moreover, the jurist Gaius wrote a commentary on them, of which some fragments survive, in which he gives us some quite extensive quotations on procedural law.

The Twelve Tables were portrayed as one result of the political struggles of the early Roman Republic. The original nature of the legal distinction between privileged patrician and unprivileged plebeian, despite much debate, remains obscure; this is partly because it was no longer of any real social or political importance after the Hortensian Act of 287 BC. It is said that the citizen body wanted restraints upon the power of magistrates, and that the humbler elements of society, the plebeians, wanted the law made public in the sense that they wished to be able to know how to use it. As Watson has pointed out,[6] the patricians responded with great political skill. The plebeians were indeed made aware of some basic rules of procedure which they would need in order to make use of the law, and some areas of substantive law were clarified, but everything in the sphere of sacral law and of constitutional power was omitted from the codification. Thus matters affecting the governance of the city-state remained in the hands of the patricians, exclusively for most of the next century, and to a considerable extent throughout the Republic. Hence also Roman private law, because it was founded in the Twelve Tables, was secular law, and religious argument played virtually no part in it. The form taken by the Twelve Tables was 'legislation', that is they were a statute – or rather two – passed by the most important of the assemblies of the Roman people, the *comitia centuriata*, and this brings us back to the constitution.

THE CONSTITUTION OF THE MIDDLE AND LATE REPUBLIC

From 366 BC until the last century BC the constitution was stable, even if its conventions were not always observed. There were three elements, magistrates, Senate, and people.[7] The magistrates exercised the executive power; they were elected annually, and each magistracy was collegiate, that is, there were two or more of each rank.[8] Any magistrate could veto (by *intercessio*) the act of his colleague(s) or of any lower magistrate; the tribunes of the people had a general power of veto. Magistrates with *imperium*, while ceasing technically to be magistrates after their year of office, could have their power prolonged; they were known as proconsuls or propraetors. The Senate was the body which advised the magistrates, and represented the majesty of the Roman people – SPQR, *Senatus Populusque Romanus*. All but the most junior magistrates already belonged to it before their term of office. The people, that is all male adult citizens,[9] met – when summoned – in various assemblies, elected the magistrates, passed (or rejected) laws proposed to them, and exercised some criminal jurisdiction.

The assemblies

All citizens had membership of the popular assemblies, whether meeting by *curiae*, by centuries or by tribes. While every citizen had a vote in each of these assemblies, not all votes were equal because, although voting was by head within each constituent group, the groups as such then cast their votes, and these groups were of different sizes. In this way even the popular element in the constitution was democratic only in a rather limited sense. Rome was, however, unusual in the ancient Mediterranean world in that, throughout the whole of Roman history, freed slaves normally became citizens, and, until quite late in the Republic, the barriers to immigrants becoming citizens were not high.

The oldest assembly was the curiate, but the nature of the thirty *curiae* which composed it remains obscure; there was some link with the clans (*gentes*), and this probably explains why the curiate assembly, presided over by the *pontifex maximus*, continued to be the forum for various legal transactions involving the family, such as will-making and adrogation (a particular form of adoption). It had some sacral functions. It also confirmed, purely formally, the election of magistrates with *imperium.*

The centuriate assembly was created later, but it was reckoned as the most important – *comitiatus maximus*, as described by Cicero.[10] It elected magistrates with *imperium*, supreme power, power of life and death over the citizens whether in war or peace (although there came to be certain restrictions on the exercise of this power). The centuriate assembly often acted as a court in capital cases. It could pass legislation, although after the Twelve Tables it did so only rarely. It also made formal declarations of war and ratified treaties of peace. It was divided into notional centuries, clearly representing the citizens in arms of the early period; these centuries were distributed among classes, theoretically based on the level of armour the citizen could afford. Although every citizen had a vote within his century, the first class and the *equites* (cavalry or equestrians)[11] together had a majority of the centuries. In the third century BC some link between the centuries and the tribes was established, but its nature is obscure.

The tribal assembly was organized originally by area; there were four urban tribes within the City and, by 241 BC, thirty-one others called rustic. Again, every citizen had a vote within his tribe, but the four urban tribes were much the largest – to them were assigned freed slaves, although a few senatorial families continued to be members – and so a vote within one of them had much less weight. The same grouping was used for meetings of the *concilium plebis*, the assembly which excluded the patrician *gentes*. Since by the later Republic the great majority of even senatorial families were technically plebeian, there was scope for confusion between the two assemblies, especially after the Hortensian Act of 287 BC had given the same force to the resolutions of this plebeian assembly (*plebiscita*) as to the legislation (*leges*) of the assemblies of the whole people. In fact most legislation of the later Republic seems to have been before the plebeian assembly, since the tribunes (*tribuni plebis*), who normally presided over it, did not, unlike the higher magistrates, have the distractions of military command or jurisdiction. Whatever the assembly, legislation was drafted by a magistrate, perhaps with the help of jurists,[12] and normally debated in the Senate; the bill (*rogatio*) was then proposed to the people who could vote only to accept or reject, without any power to amend. The tribal assembly sometimes acted as a court in non-capital trials. It also elected the lesser magistrates, without the presence of patricians for the election of the specifically plebeian magistrates, that is the plebeian aediles and the tribunes of the people.

The magistrates

The supreme executive power in the state was held by the two consuls, elected by the centuriate assembly, which was summoned by one of their predecessors (or by a dictator or *interrex* when there was no surviving consul). The consuls shared power – *imperium* – jointly; it included the supreme military command, jurisdiction, the proposal of business to an assembly or the Senate, and whatever else might be necessary.[13] Particularly in military matters this shared power sometimes led to confusion, and it became normal for the consuls to alternate the power of commander-in-chief in the field either daily, or monthly as they did at Rome; this arrangement could be altered by agreement or by lot. Each consul, during his turn, was entitled to twelve attendants, called lictors, bearing the *fasces* (rods) and – when abroad – an axe, as symbols of his power to enforce his authority. The consuls also were eponymous, that is they gave their names to the calendar year of their office.

Jurisdiction, however, particularly civil jurisdiction, was the job of the praetor, a magistracy created in 367 BC specifically to relieve the consuls of this function. At first the praetor was viewed as a junior colleague of the consuls; he too was elected by the centuriate assembly and exercised *imperium*, but was entitled to only six lictors, and his acts could be vetoed by a consul. After 242 BC the praetorship became properly collegiate when, because there had been such an increase in litigation, a second praetor was created to exercise jurisdiction over foreigners (peregrines), and, later, also in actions between citizen and foreigner.[14] The very existence of such a magistrate is a remarkable demonstration not only of Rome's growth but also of her openness. Thereafter the senior praetor (the one who had most votes) was called the Urban Praetor and the other the Peregrine Praetor. Because the praetorship necessarily gave the holder *imperium*, for military reasons the number of praetors was enlarged, to four in 227 BC and to six in

197 BC, as Rome acquired provinces which needed governors. Sulla used them to preside over his system of criminal courts, while sending out governors to the provinces with proconsular or propraetorian *imperium*. We shall return in the next chapter to the Urban Praetor, the one meant when there is reference simply to the praetor.

Below the praetors, and without *imperium*, were the aediles. The two plebeian aediles, whose office went back to the early Republic, were elected by the *concilium plebis*; two more, the curule aediles, elected by the tribal assembly, were created in the reforms of 367 BC. In spite of their different origins, the four operated as a college. Their chief concern was the *cura urbis*, the local administration of the City.[15] This involved certain police functions, including supervision of the market place, over which there came to be a civil jurisdiction exercised by the curule aediles; this was important in the development of the law of sale.

Below the aediles were the quaestors, elected by the tribal assembly. They were essentially auxiliary, acting as assistants to higher magistrates, such as consuls or provincial governors. However, the two senior quaestors, the urban quaestors or *quaestores aerarii*, exercised some independent financial functions (including the sale of state property) which were usually authorized by the Senate as well as the consuls. There were eight of them before Sulla, twenty after; before Sulla the quaestorship did not lead to (virtually) automatic membership of the Senate, but afterwards it did.

Below the senatorial magistracies were certain offices held normally by those who aspired to membership of the Senate; these were minor magistracies compared with the others, but they were held by young men of the upper ranks of society, of senatorial or ambitious equestrian family. All were elected by the tribal assembly. There were *tresviri monetales*, created in 289 BC to supervise the mint. There were six commissioners for the roads, four in Rome and two in the vicinity, who worked under the aediles. From at least the later third century BC[16] there were the *tresviri capitales*, also known as the *tresviri nocturni*, a college of three whose task was to check fires and who exercised police powers and a minor criminal jurisdiction. There were four prefects (*praefecti Capuam Cumas*) delegated to exercise the Praetor's jurisdiction in those cities, and a commission of ten (*decemviri slitibus iudicandis*) who, by the beginning of the Empire, presided over the centumviral court,[17] but earlier seem to have acted as judges in cases involving claims to free status. All these offices were known collectively as the vigintisexvirate.

Outside this hierarchy, dating from the fifth century BC, there were the two censors, senior in dignity but lacking *imperium*. They were elected, by the centuriate assembly, normally from among those who had held the consulship. Although they were a college of two, they were not annual like other magistrates but were elected every five years to exercise their office for as long as it took – and in any case no more than eighteen months; their function was not seen as needing to be permanent. Their duty was to hold the census, which assigned men to their class in society, and to fill vacancies in the Senate. They had some discretion in making these assessments, which included the power to reduce someone to a lower class, or to expel him from the Senate for conduct of which they disapproved; they could also in effect fine him by altering his tax liability. This power was by no means always exercised disinterestedly, and it usually showed a strongly conservative tendency; however, the censors had to give a reason for their *nota* (mark of censure), and either could veto the other. They were also responsible for letting out public contracts, whether for public works or the collection of taxes.[18]

Springing from the struggle of the orders between patricians and plebeians in the earlier Republic was the office of tribune of the people, not strictly a magistracy. The ten tribunes were the representatives of the people, and therefore elected by the *concilium plebis*, with specific power to aid any citizen or veto any magistrate's action. This wide-ranging (but technically irresponsible) remit seems originally to have sprung from the plebeians' forcible self-help, almost civil war, against the patricians; the tribunes were protected by personal inviolability (*sacrosanctitas*) while in office. While all this was historically based in the interests of the plebeians against the oppression of the patricians, it came to be an instrument in the political strife between *optimates* and *populares*[19] in the later Republic. Moreover, by that period, the tribunes (although required to be of plebeian family) came from the same milieu as the magistrates proper, they acquired the automatic right to a seat in the Senate, and they frequently went on to hold magistracies in the ordinary sequence of office-holding (*cursus honorum*). Further, they were responsible for much legislation, which they could propose to the *concilium plebis* or the tribal assembly, and they could convene the Senate.

Outside the hierarchy in a rather different way was the dictatorship; this was an office which harked back to the monarchy. In an emergency a consul – not the people, not the Senate – could nominate a (sole) dictator who, for his maximum six-month period of office, was supreme, superior in his *imperium* to the consuls as well as all other magistrates, as symbolized by his twenty-four lictors. The traditional dictator was not subject to the tribunician veto, but the office disappeared after 202 BC. The dictatorships of Sulla and Julius Caesar were outside the conventions of the Republican constitution, merely cloaks for their arbitrary powers which were based on military force.

The Senate

The third element of the constitution was the Senate. Its role was the least clearly defined, but was perhaps the most important in the Republican constitution. It seems to have originated as the king's council and continued to be, in theory, that of the consuls. In the Republic it had about 300 members, until Sulla's reforms doubled its size. Its membership was originally chosen by the consuls, then by the censors, but by the third century it was the convention for ex-curule (non-plebeian) magistrates to enter the Senate, and the other aediles and tribunes soon followed; after Sulla, even quaestors were entitled to membership. This right of ex-magistrates to a – lifelong – seat in the Senate will, most of the time, have kept the numbers up, so that the censors' role was probably often more negative than positive, more concerned with expulsion than enrolment.

Constitutionally, if both consuls died suddenly or were killed, the patricians in the Senate appointed an *interrex*, who had power to summon the centuriate assembly to hold consular elections. The Senate also assigned to magistrates below the consuls – to them they offered what was formally advice – their sphere of office. The Senate could declare a state of emergency, as in the Bacchanalian affair of 186 BC[20] or the Catiline conspiracy of 63 BC[21] but, certainly in the later Republic, this was a power used for party political purposes rather than as the constitutional safeguard Cicero so grandly proclaimed. It was the Senate in effect which decided on questions of war and peace, although the centuriate assembly must play its formal part; it was 'the Senate and People of Rome' which authorized or ratified peace treaties. Particularly in foreign affairs, its influence as a continuous body of experienced men must clearly have been enormous. It had, moreover, real power in financial matters. Its authorization was necessary for any unusual expenditure or for raising new taxes,[22] although the censors or the urban quaestors were the executive magistrates. It controlled the budgets of all magistrates who had them: censors, consuls, provincial governors, and others; it alone could release public contractors from their liabilities.

Because in principle the Senate had technically just an advisory role, as the council of the supreme magistrates, it did not pass anything resembling legislation concerning positive rules of private law until into the Empire, when the constitution had of course changed. However, it did have a quasi-legislative role to play, even in the Republic. It could be convened by any magistrate with *imperium* or by a tribune, and this was habitually done so that it might debate magistrates' proposals before they were put to an assembly as a bill; and from the Senate floor the magistrate might take amendments. What the Senate approved – technically a *senatusconsultum*[23] – was described as a resolution of the Senate; since this could not be put into effect until accepted by a magistrate, insofar as it had technically become the magistrate's proposal, it could be vetoed by a tribune (or a higher magistrate). Like legislation by the assemblies, written copies of resolutions of the Senate were deposited in the treasury. The Senate as such did not normally exercise judicial functions in the Republic, but senators, of course, acted as *iudices* or *recuperatores* in civil suits or were members of the criminal jury courts, as we shall see in subsequent chapters.

THE 'ROMAN REVOLUTION'

It is clear that the Republic had been failing for a century before Augustus' settlement of the constitution, a settlement which marks the start of the Principate. Many different events are taken to mark the beginning of the end of the traditional Republic. Perhaps, because it is a definite date, one might choose 133 BC and the murder of Tiberius Gracchus, lynched by 'respectable' senators. To me it seems that Sulla was its destroyer, for he claimed to be a conservative, to be restoring the old virtues, and the means he took as dictator (81–79 BC) were inevitably incompatible with his aims – a greater betrayal than the changes desired by any of the *populares* such as C.Gracchus. But certainly there were a disturbing number of figures who held a power contrary to the conventions of the constitution, such as Marius, Cinna, Sulla, or Pompey, even before Julius Caesar embarked on the last act of the Republic.

Perhaps chance was also a vital factor in the constitutional change, the chance that Augustus lived so long that the changes he brought about became accepted, the base for permanent change. He did not die until AD 14 and he had assumed the title of Augustus in 27 BC, when he 'restored the Republic', and in effect founded the Empire; he had won the battle of Actium in 31 BC. Julius Caesar had crossed the Rubicon in 49 BC; the number of people living in AD 14 who had any experience of the 'free' Republic must have been tiny. But Augustus was concerned to avoid the fate of his great-uncle; his 'restored Republic' was a transitional phase, which made possible the developed Principate. The assemblies, the Senate and the magistracies all continued in theory to function as they had done before, but Augustus was consul every year until 23 BC, with proconsular *imperium* in the frontier provinces; he controlled the armies. When, in 23 BC, he gave up the consulship, he took tribunician power for life, which allowed him to summon both Senate and people, to veto any magistrate's act, and to intervene by granting his *auxilium* to any citizen who asked for his aid; it also gave him personal inviolability (*sacrosanctitas*). Further, he took over from the Senate and centuriate assembly the power to make war and peace, according to the statement of imperial powers known as the *lex de imperio Vespasiani,* which is described in the section on the developed Principate.

The jurists and the new order: the *ius respondendi*

The vast constitutional change that hindsight shows had occurred had, however, very little immediate effect on the sources of law.[24] The jurists[25] continued to give opinions on points of law, and to make more general statements in writing, which were accepted as creating law. The one novelty, according to some romanists,[26] was the *ius publice respondendi*, a right that is sometimes argued to have made binding the individual opinions of a jurist who enjoyed it. It is in the light of some views on this problem that we must look at the social background of the jurists in the period of the 'Roman revolution'. It has been argued that the jurists of the very late Republic did not have the same prestige as their predecessors.[27]

This is perhaps literally true; there came to be some recognized jurists who were not senators, such as A.Ofilius, the friend of Julius Caesar, or Trebatius Testa, the friend of Cicero (and also Labeo's blood father). But the other jurists of the period seem nearly all to have come from senatorial families, even if some were not necessarily themselves senators.[28] To take at face value the pride of 'noble' families, and some envy of them, expressed by Cicero above all, should not blind us to the pragmatic reality, as seen either from the throne or from outside the charmed circle, particularly in a period of civil disturbance when careers were cut short by proscription or battle. Only Massurius Sabinus, of all the major jurists, seems not to have been born into the upper classes, for he did not even become an equestrian until late in life. The argument that the status of jurists had declined and needed strengthening, seems a little weak;[29] they were men of the upper classes, of at least potential senatorial status. It is, on the other hand, true that accepting honours, even merely titular honours, from the emperor increased imperial influence.[30]

Our direct information is limited to two texts, one from Pomponius in the Digest, and one from Gaius in his Institutes. Pomponius (in what is generally admitted to be a corrupt or confused passage) set out to mention the most notable of those skilled in the *ius civile*;[31] he tells us that Massurius Sabinus was an equestrian and first gave opinions on behalf of the state, and that afterwards this began to be given as a privilege – it was granted him by the Emperor Tiberius.[32] In his next sentence we are told almost the same thing:

> And, as we have said in passing, before the time of Augustus the right of giving opinions on behalf of the state was not granted by emperors[!], but men who had confidence in their knowledge gave opinions to those who consulted them. Nor were such opinions normally sealed, but written to the *iudices*[33] or given in evidence. Augustus, in order that the law might have greater authority, first established that opinions might be given with his authority ... Therefore Tiberius granted to Sabinus that he might give opinions to the people, a man who only reached the equestrian order when he was almost fifty, and who was so poor he needed to live off his students.[34]

The missing sentence in s. 49 is to the effect that

from that time this began to be sought as a privilege, and so the good emperor Hadrian [117–38], when it was sought from him by men of praetorian rank that they might be allowed to give opinions, wrote back that this was by custom not to be sought but rather to be self-evident, and so he would be delighted if any who trusted his own abilities should prepare himself for giving opinions to the people.

Gaius simply says that

the opinions of the jurists are the views and advice of those to whom it has been permitted to build up the law. If all their opinions agree, then what is so held has the force of law, but if they disagree, the judge may follow whichever view he wishes; and Hadrian indicated this in a rescript.[35]

The only crux in Gaius is 'quibus permissum est iura condere'; does 'permissum' have to mean positive imperial grant or merely imperial leave to carry on? Gaius seems to be saying little more than that jurisprudence is a source of law.[36]

Hadrian seems then to have dropped the practice of marking individuals out for approval. Pomponius' reference to Augustus may be in error for his successor Tiberius, since he twice credits Tiberius with making a grant to Sabinus. It seems incredible that Augustus, after 'restoring' the Republic would do anything as crude as making legal opinions binding on his simple authority. It is hardly more likely that Tiberius would have done so, since his divergences from Augustus' policies, such as making permanent the office of Prefect of the City, mostly stemmed from his withdrawal to Capri. On the other hand, it seems quite reasonable that a man, however learned and respected by other experts, who was not even an equestrian should need some external support; and Sabinus is the only jurist for whom we have an explicit statement of a privilege being granted. It is notable that we have a lengthy inscription about the career of the renowned jurist Julian, who consolidated the Edict under Hadrian,[37] and it contains no reference to any *ius respondendi*.[38] Moreover, Justinian tells us in the preliminaries to the Digest that he wished all jurists whom he understood – however anachronistically – to have had the *ius respondendi* to be considered for inclusion, and others not.[39] Yet we find no texts of Titius Aristo, who was a member of Trajan's *consilium* and cited frequently by other jurists, and many from Pomponius who, according to various modern romanists, did not issue formal *responsa*. Further, since we know that, even in Justinian's time, there remained major areas of dispute, any imperial strengthening of the opinions of some jurists can hardly have created binding law. Any grant must have been more of the nature of an honour (rather like appointing silks – King's or Queen's Counsel – in the English tradition) than of authority, even for a particular case, although it is true that men might have been swayed by the existence of honours. And such a limited interpretation is the more likely in that the growth of imperial law-making was itself creeping. Augustus issued edicts, but as any magistrate might have done; he sat in judgment with an unspecified authority. After the period of the civil wars he does not seem to have exercised any arbitrary powers; merely his authority (moral as well as enforceable) was greater than that of any other man.[40]

THE PRINCIPATE

The Principate can be divided from the legal standpoint into several stages, first the Julio-Claudians, then the high period (Trajan, Hadrian, Antoninus Pius and Marcus Aurelius), and then the Severan dynasty; the interruptions of such 'bad' emperors as Domitian or Commodus had no impact on legal history. After that there were some fifty years of political confusion, if not chaos. In the first 250 years there were 25 emperors (including AD 69, the year of the four emperors); then in the next 50 there were again some 25. Plague, civil war, foreign invasion and plain bad luck all played their part to create instability. Then, in AD 284, Diocletian came to power; he restored equilibrium to the system, while necessarily transforming it. Judging from his legislation he was, like Augustus, essentially a conservative. The rescripts from his chancery were in the same tradition as those of a century before, cautious, practical, simple in style. It was only the reign of Constantine in the early fourth century which, for legal historians, marks the break, the change to the Dominate – to which we shall return.

New institutions

From Tiberius on there was no doubt that Rome was an autocracy. This was made the clearer by the need to delegate or formalize authority because of his absence from Rome in the latter part of his reign. The emperor was commander-in-chief of the army, *princeps senatus*, armed with permanent *imperium*, tribunician power, and, from Domitian, perpetual censorship. Although after Domitian's assassination the title of censor ceased to be used, censorial control had already become a permanent imperial function. The nature of imperial power after the end of the Julio-Claudians is described by what remains of the so-called *lex de imperio Vespasiani*:[41] the emperor had the power to make treaties, to summon the Senate and transact with it in all ways as though by statutory authority, to recommend magistrates for election, to enlarge the *pomerium*, to do whatever was according to the custom of the *res publica*, and to be exempt from or empowered to act in accordance with particular laws. The emperors had enormous private wealth, and their patrimony was used for public as well as private purposes. The old state treasury, the *aerarium*, continued to function, but the imperial treasury, called the fisc, received direct taxes from the provinces, and indirect taxes imposed at Rome, such as those on the sale of slaves or the inheritance tax.[42] As to their actual law-making power, it seems there was no strict constitutional authority; they had acquired it *de facto*. Gaius still looked for an explanation: 'because the emperor is given his *imperium* by law'[43] – hardly satisfactory reasoning. Nevertheless, the lawmaking power was undoubtedly there.

The civil service too became more formal, partly because it came to be more common for the emperor to be absent from Rome; it became slowly distinguishable from his *familia*, the extended family of slaves, freedmen and dependents.[44] By Hadrian's reign imperial freedmen had largely been replaced by men of the equestrian order. The *equites* indeed came to be primarily the class which provided professional civil and military servants; the ethos seems to have switched from commerce to service (as it did in British India between the eighteenth and nineteenth centuries), although in both cases the majority would have been concerned primarily with the management of their landed estates. Still defined in theory by a census qualification, their upper reaches were those to whom the emperor might grant the *latus clavus* (a broad purple stripe on the toga) as symbol of his permission to aspire to senatorial rank. The notion of beginning an administrative career as a military tribune or with some other military rank remained commonplace until Hadrian's reign; then under Septimius Severus junior military command or staff positions again became a regular preliminary to promotion in the public service.

Two new offices which emerged early in the Principate were to have an important part in the later administration of justice. The Prefect of the City acquired a criminal jurisdiction in the City and within a 100 mile radius of it that is evidenced for the time of Severus, but probably was considerably older; he also developed a considerable civil jurisdiction. The Praetorian Prefect or Prefects – for the office was often held by two men jointly – who was in effect the emperor's chief of staff, became frequently the emperor's delegate, because of his proximity, when there was nobody with a more specific claim. In this way the Praetorian Prefect began, again under the Severi at the latest, to exercise an appellate jurisdiction in the emperor's name; in this period legal skills seem to have been one of the qualifications for the office, for between AD 203 and 223[45] it was held by jurists such as Papinian and, more briefly, Paul and Ulpian.

The majority of the senior civil servants in the developed Empire held the rank of procurator at one level or another.[46] The office had started as an agency for the emperor, akin to the meaning of the word in private law usage, exercised by imperial freedmen, but by the later first century it was normally equestrian. Procurators, on the usual Roman principle, exercised jurisdiction within their sphere of office. Certain specific functions had their own names. The *ab epistulis* was the emperor's chief-of-office for dealing with the imperial correspondence, including letters on legal matters, and this came to include the appointment and promotion of imperial officials; it came to be divided into a Latin and a Greek section. The *a libellis* was the chief-of-office for dealing with petitions sent to the emperor; many of these asked for advice on points of law, and it is clear that legal skill became a prerequisite for the office, which was the chief source of rescripts. The *a cognitionibus* was probably also in need of legal knowledge, for he seems to have been an imperial official with judicial responsibilities.[47] The *a memoria* headed something akin to the emperor's private office.

The old: magistrates and assemblies

Magistrates continued to be elected, although the elections were under Tiberius transferred from the assemblies to the Senate; as Pliny's letters show, however, they continued to be contested, even if some particular candidate favoured by the emperor could be sure of election. The consuls also continued to give their names to the year and to preside over the Senate, and the office was often a prerequisite for later advancement in the imperial administration to provincial governorships. Praetors continued to exercise jurisdiction,[48] civil and criminal, and each year the Urban Praetor issued his edict until it was consolidated by the jurist Julian under the emperor Hadrian. The aediles also continued to exercise some jurisdiction, but their importance was clearly declining in comparison with the new officials concerned with the *cura urbis*;[49] their role in the administration of the criminal law must also have declined.[50] Modern textbooks, and indeed Gaius, talk as though civil jurisdiction was simply a matter for the Praetor, but it must have been more complicated than that; the tribunes, for instance, exercised some sort of jurisdiction.[51]

The assemblies continued to be used by the Julio-Claudians for legislation on certain matters, matters affecting marriage, tutory, and slavery, traditional areas of Roman law, where presumably the emperors wanted to use traditional means to make their changes more acceptable. However, while it has been argued that the last comitial law was in 96, it seems more probable that no assembly ever met after AD 68, except notionally to hear the results of the elections made by the Senate.[52] The Senate took over their legislative as it had taken over their electoral role. SCC began regularly to be concerned with private law matters, whereas in the Republic they had nearly always been concerned with public law – including criminal law under this head. The force of the resolutions of the Senate in making law was the emperor's approval, even if in early days the phraseology was still a recommendation to him as the successor of the consuls.[53] But, as I have argued elsewhere,[54] although the political role of the Senate had naturally disappeared, it is most misleading to say it simply rubber-stamped what the emperor wanted; it remained a highly influential body. The full Senate (of some 600 men) was, however, really too large a body to act as the emperor's council, and there developed an inner or privy council, the *consilium principis*. For long this was an informal body of the emperor's friends; it may have begun to take institutional form under Hadrian, with some members being salaried, but, like the constitution in general, it was a matter of convention rather than rigid requirement.[55] By the end of the second century it normally included the various Prefects and the office chiefs.[56]

THE LATER EMPIRE

Diocletian made changes to the constitution, with a division of the Empire into western and eastern halves, but Constantine changed its nature more profoundly, and not only because he legalized Christianity, of which he was himself an adherent. The imperial dignity became a sacred matter; the emperor was no longer theoretically first among equals (*princeps inter pares*)[57] but a remote and sacred figure, surrounded by ceremonial. Although the cult of emperor as god began to die out, it was replaced, at a deeper (because less incredible) level, by the emperor as God's agent.

Diocletian's administrative reorganization provisionally put all the Empire on the same footing. In the Later Empire, that is administratively (although not jurisprudentially) from the reign of Diocletian, there was no specific Roman law distinct from what was available in the provinces; even Italy no longer had a special status. The new administrative structure split up the traditional provinces; for example at one stage there were five where there had been one in Britain.[58] Each group of these new provinces was classed as a diocese, nearly always under a vicar, and the dioceses grouped into four (Praetorian) Prefectures (Oriens, Illyria, Italy, Gaul) – two for the East, two for the West. The cities of Rome, and shortly Constantinople, with their surroundings, were alone outside the new structure. The Praetorian Prefects no longer acted as the emperor's delegates but *vice sacra*, in his stead; this change in the importance of their role was partly because the creation of the *magistri militum* by Constantine had separated civil from military office.[59] They now headed the whole civil administration, with all the jurisdictional powers which the logic of Roman thought implied. The Praetorian Prefects and the Prefects of the City of the two capitals held the topmost rank of *illustris*, as did the *quaestor* (*sacri palatii* as he became frequently known), the *magister officiorum*, and the two treasury chiefs (*comites sacrarum largitionum* and *rerum privatarum*). The quaestor was a minister of justice, with the duty of drafting legislation and answering petitions; thus he took over the functions of the *a memoria* and the *a libellis*, but without himself having an office staff – or only a skeleton one.[60] The *magister officiorum* was the head of all the civil service departments (*scrinia*), whose chiefs were now responsible to him rather than the emperor. The imperial council became the *consistorium*, 'probably because the members stood, while the emperor alone sat',[61] but its existence was still based on convention. Of all its functions the judicial seems to have remained the most important. Rather like the American civil and foreign services, the very top ranks of the Later Roman administration seem often to have been filled as political appointments, leaving a deeply entrenched permanent bureaucracy up to approximately the (British) Deputy Secretary level; these officials were often held responsible for any wrongful actions of their superior. We have a wonderful account in the *de magistratibus* of John Lydus, a senior civil servant under Justinian.[62] Another change was that the old equestrian order disappeared, but officials of a similar status came to be known as *perfectissimi* or *comites* of the first, second or third rank; members of the learned professions might be recognized as *comites* of the third rank. These titles were of importance in that they, even more than general membership of the class of *honestiores*, which still included the decurion class,[63] carried exemption from certain burdens, gave more weight to someone's evidence, and normally provided immunity from torture.[64]

Diocletian's division of the Empire into two halves did not become really effective until the best part of a century later, after the end of Constantine's dynasty, but from AD 395 it was a permanent fact, with some awkward legal consequences – such as the problem of making legislation effective in the 'other' half. Imperial enactments can be difficult to interpret when it is not clear which emperor was actually responsible, or when the emperor was in fact merely the mouthpiece of his tutors or advisers. The flow was mostly from East to West; in particular, Theodosius II, emperor in the East, had his Code promulgated by Valentinian III in the West. The Empire in the West effectively came to an end in 455 after the murder of Valentinian (who was grandson of Theodosius I), which led to the sack of Rome by the Vandals; the conventional ending, however, is often given as 476, with the deposition of Orestes' puppet, Romulus Augustulus, by Odoacer.[65] Thereafter there was a single emperor, at Constantinople, until Justinian's reconquest of some of the West through his generals, first Belisarius and then Narses. But in the West the Germanic invaders admired the written law of Rome, as well as adopting Christianity. As they settled they took notice of the Theodosian Code, and of the various legal epitomes and handbooks which were current in the West, and they preserved much of them, often by incorporation into their new codes, such as the *Edict* of Theoderic, Alaric's *Lex Romana Visigothorum* of 506, or the *Lex Romana Burgundionum* of Gundobad.[66]

Lawmaking in the Later Empire

In the period after Diocletian the jurists disappeared, in the sense that there were no longer men of high rank skilled in legal science, whose opinions had authority on their intellectual merits and peer recognition, as well as from imperial approval. They survived indeed as the senior legal advisers to the emperor and as the professors of law in the law schools of the Later Empire, but the only legal authority was that of the emperor.[67] Legal opinions were given by the quaestor in the emperor's name; all judicial decisions were given by the emperor's inferiors, from whom appeal was almost always possible; all positive legislation, in the sense of direct lawmaking, came from the emperor. It is not surprising that Justinian's understanding of the *ius respondendi* and the whole role of the jurists was somewhat peculiar; the world had changed.

Society had changed, and the constitution had changed; although the link was not necessarily close, it is not surprising that the authority of the sources of law had also changed. Nor is it deplorable that the case law of the Republic and Principate gave way to the general legislation of the Later Empire. It was necessary. The vast output of the classical period needed pruning. Under Diocletian a start was made with the *Codex Gregorianus*, which collected imperial rescripts apparently from the reign of Hadrian until its present;[68] it was divided into books and titles, probably in the traditional arrangement of the Praetor's Edict,[69] with criminal and public law at the end. The *Codex Hermogenianus* was presumably a supplement, bringing the law up to date for rather later in Diocletian's reign; there seem to have been further editions, for some further enactments were added almost a century later. Both codes were probably published in the East under Diocletian's auspices.

Nearly a century and a half later Theodosius II tried to produce another systematic statement of the law in force. His project for a collection of juristic writings to be blended with imperial enactments never got off the ground,[70] but his Code was published in 438; it contained imperial legislation only from Constantine, perhaps deliberately from the Christian emperors. Further, unlike the earlier codes, it was restricted to general edicts, statutory law.

Included in this Code was an enactment from 426, commonly known as the Law of Citations.[71] To simplify the use of juristic writings, this gave prime authority to five classical jurists, Papinian, Ulpian, Paul, Modestinus, and Gaius, and secondary to jurists cited by the five, provided the texts were checked. As Jolowicz says,[72] the reason was presumably the availability of the manuscripts of the four most modern jurists and of the currently popular Gaius; also, of course, their law would be most up to date. A majority opinion where there was disagreement was, not unreasonably,[73] to prevail; if there was a dispute but no majority, then Papinian's view was to prevail, failing which the judge must use his discretion.

Justinian

Justinian, almost a century later, again decided to codify the law. His work has been of enormous importance, because it has shaped the whole development of European law, and of law wherever western Europeans founded colonies. It is also of enormous importance to our understanding and interpretation of the sources of Roman law because it is almost entirely through this that we have what we are able to know of the great bulk of Roman law. Justinian's legislation was designed to supplant all earlier laws, whether imperial enactments or the legal writings of the jurists, the two forms which had survived into the third century. In the East it seems that this was almost entirely successful;[74] in the West much less so, because Justinian's work was not promulgated there until after the recovery of Italy from the Ostrogoths,[75] when the Franks and the Visigoths were already well settled in what were to become France and Spain. His reformed law was not only too late but also too complex and sophisticated for the Germanic settlers to absorb, and so it was not received in the West, not until the renaissance of learning in the eleventh and twelfth centuries. But that is another story, the story of the second life of Roman law.[76]

Justinian's codification, as it has survived to us, consists of the Institutes, an elementary work for first-year law students, the Digest, an edited collection of juristic writings, the Code, an edited collection of imperial enactments which included many of the general laws found in the Theodosian Code, but which was not confined to general edicts and which went back to Hadrian, and finally – although never officially collected – Justinian's subsequent legislation, known as his Novels. The Institutes were heavily based on those of Gaius, some three and a half centuries earlier, but also explicitly used Gaius' *Res Cottidianae* and elementary works or epitomes from, among others, Marcian, Florentinus, Paul, and Ulpian. The Digest is of particular interest because the compilers were ordered to leave at the head of each extract the name of its author and the provenance, e.g. Ulpian, book 7 *ad Sabinum*. The Code too preserved the names of the emperors, the dates of their enactments and the addressees; even if not always accurate, this is a start for modern students. The Novels do not concentrate on private law, as do the other parts of the codification, but deal with a whole range of matters, including the administrative and ecclesiastical; they are often equivalent to a consolidating statute. These works, known to us as the *Corpus Iuris Civilis*, will be discussed more fully in chapters 3 and 4; the Novels, however, will be touched on only lightly, as they mark the foundation of Byzantine law and they had little influence on subsequent legal development in western Europe. Here it is enough to say that there was an earlier Code, published in 529, but found unsatisfactory for reasons that remain uncertain. It is possible that originally Justinian intended simply an updated Theodosian Code but that, as work on the Digest progressed, the need was seen to include rescripts from the Principate in order to put in context the writings of the jurists.[77] Justinian also issued the so-called Fifty Decisions, settling points which had long been in dispute, but we do not know what these fifty were; they were overtaken by events. Nor do we know if they were issued because Justinian thought that would be sufficient, with the Law of Citations, to allow sensible use of juristic writings, or whether he had already determined on the Digest but was providing an interim measure. The Institutes and Digest were published together in 533, and the new version of the Code in 534. With the issue of these three we can say, in one sense, that the history of Roman law has come to its conclusion.

NOTES

1 The last *interrex* held office in 52 BC but the office of *rex sacrorum* lasted well into the Empire (CIL IX 2847; XIV 3604).

2 See FIRA i c.I = ARS no. 1.

3 Schulz (1953), p. 89f., but see Watson (1972a), who holds that they do conform to the reality of early law.

4 Livy 3.34.6. See *Roman Statutes*, pp. 555–721, for the most recent critical text with commentary.

5 Cicero *de leg.* 2.23.59.

6 Watson (1992), especially chs 2 & 3.

7 Polybius 6.5.11–18 explains the balance of the powers.

8 The praetor created in 367 BC was an exception until 242 BC, but he was during that period viewed as a junior colleague of the consuls, since he also exercised *imperium* – which will shortly be defined.

9 At Rome, unlike some Greek states, women were truly citizens, but they could not participate in the sphere of public law.

10 Cicero *de leg.* 3.4.11; 3.19.44.

11 The equestrians came to be ranked (by wealth) as a specific class below senatorials, but originally they may have been senators' sons. There was clearly overlap between the two, and fairly frequent inter-marriage.

12 Their role will be explained later in this chapter.

13 E.g. attending at fires, as Cicero claimed, *in Pis.* 11.26.

14 Daube (1951).

15 Robinson (1994), *passim.*

16 They were known to Plautus, e.g. *Aulul.* 416ff; *Asin.* 130–2.

17 See ch. 4.

18 Polybius 6.5.17.

19 The better sort and the popular party – a difference somewhat akin to American Republicans and Democrats.

20 See Livy 39.8–19.

21 See, for a recent account of the Catiline conspiracy, Wiseman (1994) at pp. 353–60.

22 After 168 BC direct taxation was not imposed on Roman citizens during the Republic.

23 Abbreviated to SC; SCC is the plural, *senatusconsulta.*

24 'In general changes [in legal history] come gradually, lagging rather behind economic and social developments, and it is only after a long time has elapsed that we can see how great the transformation has been. Moreover, constitutional changes, such as that from republic to empire, may have very little effect on the private law.' Jolowicz, 4–5.

25 Their history and authority is explained in ch. 2; their role will also be discussed more fully in later chapters.

26 The normal term for academic lawyers who study Roman law.

27 Kunkel (1967); but he classes as humble – or almost – men from equestrian families who went on to achieve magistracies, which is true only from a very high senatorial perspective.

28 See the list in Schulz (1953), pp. 46–8.

29 Remember that only some 600 men, and their immediate families, were senatorial in an age when the – admittedly total, including slaves – population of the City of Rome was around a million, and all Italy was citizen. Crook (1994a), at pp. 553–4, agrees that Kunkel's attitude to rank is somewhat unreal.

30 As was pointed out to me by Alan Watson.

31 D 1.2.2.35, Pomponius *enchiridion.*

32 D 1.2.2.48, *ibid.*

33 The 'judges' were in effect jurymen, not trained lawyers; see ch. 4.

34 D 1.2.2.49 & 50, Pomponius *enchiridion.*

35 G 1.7.

36 Cf. D 1.1.7, Papinian 2 *defin*; 1.2.2.12, Pomponius *enchiridion*; Cicero *Topica* 5.28. See ch. 2; see also de Zulueta (1953), 21ff.

37 See ch. 2.

38 ILS 8973 = CIL VIII 24094.

39 *Deo auctore* 4.

40 This is why it is unlikely that he made any prescriptive change to the moral authority that jurists as a class already exercised.

41 FIRA i no. 15, 154f = ARS no. 183; see also *Roman Statutes*, pp. 549–53. The first part is missing; it presumably dealt with the emperor's tribunician power and his proconsular *imperium*.

42 Jones (1950).

43 G. 1.5.

44 Jones (1949); Weaver (1972).

45 This has been the date accepted since 1967 by the *communis opinio* for the death of Ulpian; however, there is a strong argument for the restoration of 228 in Bauman (1995).

46 Consider that in most British ministries, the top civil servant is the Secretary, then Deputy Secretary, Under Secretary, Assistant Secretary. . . . Of the imperial procurators there were some *trecenarii*, who received an annual salary of HS 300,000, and below them *ducenarii* (HS 200,000), *centenarii* (HS 100,000) and *sexagenarii* (HS 60,000).

47 This was the view of Premerstein (1900); Bleicken (1962), at pp. 109–10, thought he dealt with personal petitions.

48 As will be described more fully in chs 2 & 4.

49 Robinson (1994), *passim*.

50 Tacitus *Annals* 13.28.

51 Tacitus *Annals* 13.28, at end; *Histories* IV.9; Juvenal 7.228; cf. D 50.13.1.14, Ulpian 8 *de omn.trib.*, which may originally have referred to tribunes rather than praetors.

52 Dio 58.20.4.

53 The attempted distinction between comitial legislation and SCC based on the latter's advisory form can easily be over-stressed; in either case it was necessary for the executive arm, a magistrate, to put the law into effect.

54 Robinson (1996).

55 See Philo, *Legatum ad Gaium*, at chs 11 & 18; see also Crook (1955).

56 Cf. Dio's anachronistic record of Maecenas' advice to Augustus on the nature of his *consilium* (52.33.3).

57 Unlike the story of Hadrian at the public baths – SHA *Hadrian* 17; cf. too how modern democratic royalty chose to ride bicycles, before security became an issue.

58 Gaul south of the Loire (the future Languedoc) was now a diocese, with seven to eleven provinces. See *Notitia Dignitatum*, pp. 170–1, or the map on p. 176 of Talbert (1985).

59 Although military terminology was now used to describe civil servants who, if they were sons in paternal power, became entitled to a *peculium quasi-castrense* – a personal fund which they could administer in much the same way as a soldier-son.

60 Harries (1988), especially pp. 159–64.

61 Jolowicz, 428.

62 He retired as *cornicularius*, the deputy chief, from the Praetorian Prefecture of the Oriens in 552, having made 2000 *solidi* in this last year of his forty-year career; see also Bandy (1983; Caimi (1984); Maas (1992).

63 But CJ 10.32.38, AD 384; 10.34.1, AD 386; CTh 16.2.39, AD 408; 12.1.181, AD 416; etc.

64 These privileges were also extended to their immediate families; the bulk of the population could be described as *humiliores*, the humbler sort.

65 Described as 'one of the most famous non-events in history' by Cameron (1993), at p. 33; cf. Croke (1983).

66 See ch. 3.

67 CJ 1.14.1, AD 316.

68 Although the earliest dated enactment in it (that has survived to us) is as late as 196, it must have included much earlier rescripts, since Justinian acknowledged it as the source for his Code, which goes back to Hadrian.

69 This was unsystematic; it began and finished with procedural matters, but, for instance, contracts based on good faith followed the liability of shipowner for his shipmaster and preceded dotal property. See Lenel (1927) and, for an outline, Schulz (1953), pp. 149f.

70 CTh 1.1.5, AD 429.

71 CTh 1.4.3, AD 426.

72 Jolowicz, 452.

73 There is nothing deplorable in such a method in an age when there were no longer jurists to argue with their predecessors.

74 The *scholia Sinaitica* and the *Syro-Roman Lawbook* are the principal exceptions. They are printed in FIRA ii pp. 635–52, and 751–98, where the latter is edited by J.Furlani; see also Selb (1990).

75 The pragmatic sanction of 554 put the Novels into force (App. 7 to Novels, s. 11), but it is not clear how long, or how effectively, the Digest and the Code had been law in the West.

76 ELH, *passim*.

77 P.Oxy. XV 1814 gives an apparent list of the rubrics of the later titles of Book I of this first Code; see de Francisci (1922); Krüger (1922).

Chapter 2

The Legal Sources

THE SOURCES DEFINED

A 'source' of law, in the lawyer's sense, is that to which someone –
whether judge, legislator, jurist, law agent, or private individual
– goes to find out what the law is. The primary source of modern
western law is statute. Indeed, a source of law is most commonly,
both in Roman and in modern law, something in writing, but
it need not be; for example, for both Cicero and modern Scots
law, equity is a source of law. Moreover, the writing may record an
oral statement of the law. Of course, oral law in the true sense is
constantly giving way to written law, because unless the decisions
are written down a custom is no more reliable than a man's
memory, as Robert de Beaumanoir remarked in the thirteenth
century.[1] In a similar way, the use of judicial precedent, of looking
to previous decisions made in similar cases to the instant one – a
technical term for the case currently before a particular court
– is dependent on knowing what these previous decisions were.
It only became usable as an objective source, going beyond an
individual's memory, once there were regular written law reports.

We are fortunate in having three independent statements of
what the sources of Roman law were, one from Cicero in the late
Republic (earlier last century BC),[2] one from the jurist Gaius (who
was probably a law professor) in the later second century AD,[3]
and one from the Emperor Justinian (AD 527–65).[4] The three
statements have much in common, although their purposes, and
indeed their authority, were rather different; none of them gives
any order of priority to the sources. Their variations are explicable,
as we shall see. Cicero's list is: equity, custom, decided cases,
legislation (the *leges* of the assemblies, mentioned in the previous
chapter, including those of the plebeian assembly), resolutions of

the Senate, edicts of magistrates, and the decisions of the jurists. Gaius listed legislation, resolutions of the Senate, edicts of magistrates, imperial enactments (*constitutiones*), and decisions of the jurists. Justinian followed Gaius, but added custom to his list. Both Gaius and Justinian classified these sources as coming from *ius civile*, the law of the city state of Rome, or from the *ius gentium*, the laws found (even if in differing versions) among all peoples; Justinian also referred to natural law, although this was narrowly defined, as hardly more than instinct. Cicero saw his sources as defining the *ius civile*, which he understood as meaning private law, the law used in disputes between citizens, as opposed to public law. (This is yet another indication of the regular bias towards private law, which is what the Romans implicitly meant when they referred to 'law'.) *Seems a tendentious reading of Cicero.*

EQUITY

Equity was listed by Cicero because he was an orator rather than a lawyer. He must have had (despite his disclaimers) a considerable knowledge of the law, but his business was always to present a case (usually, but not always, the defence) and so he was making use of law rather than defining or developing it. In talking to a jury, an appeal to what is equitable is attractive, particularly if the letter of the law seems against you. In Crook's words, equity, like custom, 'was not so much a source of law as a principle by which cases could be judged and the law be interpreted and developed'.[5] We also find some references to equity in the juristic writing of Cicero's time.[6] Both Gaius and Justinian will undoubtedly have recognized equity or justice as necessarily the aim of law, but they were concerned with the means, the methods a student must learn, to find the law, and so they omitted it from their lists, which come from their elementary student textbooks. Justinian opened the Digest, however, with the statement that law (*ius*) was derived from justice, the *ars boni et aequi*, as Celsus had defined it;[7] he also began the Institutes with the statement: 'Justice is the constant and permanent will that each should receive what is his due'.[8] We can find some influence from Greek philosophy – even if not any direct philosophical influence – in such definitions, and also in Justinian's reference to natural law, although Greek influence on the jurists seems to have been part of their general culture rather than specific. Further, both Gaius and Justinian saw good faith as an integral part of most procedure – as we shall see in chapter 4, on the settling of disputes.

DECIDED CASES

Decided cases, again, were listed by the orator, not the lawyers – as it seems reasonable in the context to class both Gaius and Justinian, despite the inevitably great difference between a law professor and an emperor. Cicero appealed to the recent memory of the juries he was addressing; they would remember that a decision had gone this way in a case whose facts were very similar to the instant case. As we have remarked, decided cases, precedent, cannot be a reliable source of law until it is possible to ascertain not only the judgment but also the facts on which it was based, and without something approaching what we know as law reports, such certainty is impossible beyond living memory. There may, however, be some overlap with custom here, since custom can be constructed from decided cases.[9] The Romans did not have law reports, although collections of decided cases seem to have been made in Egypt.[10] Moreover, in the older forms of procedure the judge (*iudex*) who gave the decision was not a trained lawyer but a layman, trying a case after the issues of law had been settled before the Praetor, so there was no innate authority in such decisions. The emperors issued their authoritative opinions on facts put before them, but they constantly added the caution that their view of the law was dependent on the truth of these facts, and so was rather a statement of the law in isolation than a binding precedent. Further it was not always clear whether a decision was for a particular case only or to have general application.[11] Away from central records, such as they were, other Romans exercising judicial office, such as provincial governors, had even less chance of knowing the law from previous cases.[12] In the Later Empire, it was the personal nature of rescripts which put their validity in doubt; there was no way to check on the facts alleged.[13] Justinian attempted to give authority to imperial decisions for all similar cases, but the difficulties led him to warn judges to seek truth and justice through general laws.[14]

CUSTOM

Custom was listed by both Cicero and Justinian, but not by Gaius. Again, Cicero the orator was used to appealing to a jury to preserve good Roman usage; custom for him was *mores maiorum*, ancestral tradition. It, like equity, was an appeal to the emotions of his auditors, who must be persuaded to take his side. In Cicero's time Roman law, applicable to Roman citizens, was valid in Rome and all Italy – after 90 BC south of the Po and after 49 BC south of the Alps – and in only a few communities elsewhere. Thus custom was a reasonably coherent concept; there must have been many usages familiar to most Italians. For example, the Roman concept of paternal power seems simply a customary growth, with no specific origin; it was not, for example, ascribed to the laws of the kings. Again, the prohibition on gifts between husband and wife existed *moribus*, through custom. Custom also seems to lie behind the classification of *pecudes* in ch. 1 of the *lex Aquilia*.[15] While the number of individual citizens and of communities enjoying the privilege of Roman law did, of course, increase, there was, nevertheless, no fundamental change in the sphere of Roman law for some three centuries; the Roman world of Gaius was still largely centred on Italy. Custom, however, did not appear to Gaius as an independent source of law because for him it was subsumed in the interpretation of the jurists.[16] Custom, in the direct sense of what people actually do, coming to influence the law, to make law, had had no more reality in Cicero's time than that of Gaius; custom as understood before the Praetor was not social observance but what the jurists accepted as so traditional as not to need any specific authority.[17] The kind of custom external to such interpretation presumably included customs of a trade, for example the measure used to pour away uncollected wine when the seller had need of his tanks for the new season's wine;[18] local custom obviously existed,[19] but for Gaius it was not to the point.

The situation changed when, in AD 212, the emperor Antoninus Severus, more commonly known as Caracalla, extended citizenship to (virtually) all free inhabitants of the Empire by the *constitutio Antoniniana*. This Roman Empire comprised all of the Mediterranean basin,[20] Asia Minor, the Balkan states, central Europe, and western Europe – excluding Scandinavia and northern Germany, Ireland and Scotland; the frontier lay roughly on the line of the Rhine and the Danube, with the province of Raetia filling in the corner.

The interesting question of how far all these new-made citizens did actually use the technicalities of Roman law is beyond the scope of this book. By the time of Justinian, three hundred and more years later, the African provinces had been much reduced, the Persians were pressing on the eastern frontier, and Germanic peoples had settled in most of the western provinces, but the Empire he ruled was a conglomerate still, and his list recognized that there must be many local customs.[21] Custom for Justinian was thus not the traditions of the Romans, whether unwritten or having no identifiable origin, but reasonable local deviations from the 'Roman' law that was the *ius commune* of the whole empire, such as the nature of security when land was sold or the scope of a tutor's duties.[22]

LEGISLATION: *LEGES* AND *PLEBISCITA*

Legislation covered both the *leges* of the assemblies of the whole Roman people and the *plebiscita* of the plebeian assembly; the latter was in fact the form of the vast majority of the known private law statutes. The term *lex* in normal usage covered both forms, as with the *lex Aquilia*. Legislation was a binding source of law for all three of our lists. Again, there is a difference between Cicero and the other two, but this time it is because for Cicero legislation was still happening; indeed he was responsible for a Tullian Act on electoral corruption.[23] Augustus made considerable use of legislation, particularly in such traditional areas as family law (in the wider sense); he preferred to have his later statutes passed by the centuriate assembly on the proposal of the consuls, but *plebiscita* were also used, as they were under Claudius. This revival of the centuriate assembly may be the explanation of why Gaius, and Justinian echoing him, should make a distinction between *leges* and *plebiscita*, a distinction which had been unreal since the *lex Hortensia* of 287 BC.[24] The assemblies ceased, however, to pass legislation during the course of the first century, probably around the end of the Julio-Claudian dynasty. Even for Gaius it was a source that had not been active for perhaps a century; for Justinian there had been no *leges* passed for nearly half a millennium.

Lex, statute, had been the supreme, the sovereign, statement of law, even although it was apparently not a method much used for the development of private law. This relatively meagre use of legislation seems best explained by the weight given at the time of the Twelve Tables to pontifical juristic interpretation and, later, to the flexibility of the Praetor's remedies. The best known example of a statute, with a long subsequent history, is probably the *lex Aquilia* on wrongfully caused financial loss. The first chapter laid down:

> Whoever kills wrongfully another's male or female slave or fourfooted animal or animal of the grazing class, shall be condemned to give the owner as much money as was its highest value in the last year.[25]

The second chapter had fallen into desuetude, but the third said:

> Concerning other property, aside from the killing of a slave or grazing animal, if anyone shall cause financial loss to another, by burning, breaking, or damaging wrongfully, he shall be condemned to pay as much money as the matter shall turn out to be worth in the next thirty days.[26]

This covered someone who injured a slave or grazing animal, or who killed or injured, destroyed or damaged, any other living or inanimate property belonging to someone else. Such legislation, where not repealed, continued in force for the whole life of Roman law. Justinian's codification shows that the rules laid down by, for example, the Junian Act on informally freed slaves (until he repealed it) or the Falcidian Act regulating the shares of an inheritance taken by heirs and legatees were, just like the Aquilian Act, still in force in his day. Assembly legislation continued to be the basis of criminal law too,[27] whereas most of the many political enactments of the Republic had, naturally, long ceased to have any relevance.

There were also laws, sometimes known by us as *leges datae*, which sometimes were comitial laws, but were also perhaps issued by a magistrate with *imperium*, and certainly later by the emperor. These are the kind of laws which provide a charter for a colony or municipality; the best example is perhaps the *lex Irnitana*.[28] A special kind of legislation was that performed by the *comitia calata*, an assembly of the *curiae* under the presidency of the *pontifex maximus*, which in the early Republic had been used for making wills. Because of the implications for sacral law of the ending of a particular family, when a male not in paternal power was to be adopted – technically known as adrogation – this assembly also legislated for such an adoption, after pontifical investigation; this practice continued into the Empire.[29]

The Twelve Tables had a special place as the 'source and origin of all our law'.[30] It was the pontifical and juristic interpretation of the Twelve Tables that comprised the *ius civile* in the narrow sense, the *ius civile* as opposed to the *ius honorarium* developed by, or through, the Praetor. Since the Praetor controlled almost the whole private law, directly through his jurisdictional function and indirectly because his Edict indicated the categories and limits of available remedies, the narrow *ius civile* had already been absorbed into the law as actually administered as early as the beginnings of the Empire; nevertheless, jurists in the third century, and Justinian in the sixth, continued to make a meaningless distinction.[31] Further, many of the techniques of interpretation found suitable in the period of the Twelve Tables continued to be applied to later legislation, including the Senate's resolutions and the explicit lawmaking of the emperors, so in this sense the influence of the Twelve Tables far outlasted the particular rules they laid down.[32]

The majority of statutes passed were not concerned with private law. Far more dealt with public law, or with sacral law, or with immediate political concerns – such as agrarian laws, the granting of extraordinary honours, or debt release. Legislation generally was reactive, providing a solution for a particular problem or injustice, not creating social policy. There were adequate mechanisms elsewhere for the normal requirements of developing the law. The probability seems that we have a reasonably reliable knowledge of legislation on private law, despite Cicero's claim that there were innumerable statutes on the civil law.[33] There are unlikely to be many complete omissions, because there are not many areas where simple juristic interpretation or the steady work of the Praetor cannot explain changes in the law, and because juristic opinions, which habitually refer to relevant legislation, do not themselves seem to have significant gaps. Nevertheless, much of legislation in general must have disappeared, or there would have been no need for Caesar to have proposed the publication of an official collection – his assassination prevented the completion of the project.

Further, while most legislation dealt with passing matters, what was enacted on private law was more likely to have a formal and permanent nature. Such legislation was likely to be inscribed on stone or bronze. All legislation was normally published, that is posted, written in black on white-painted wood or engraved on stone or bronze, although publication was not technically necessary for its validity. An official copy might be kept in the state treasury, the *aerarium*, but clearly not in any organized way. Laws were probably drafted either by jurists (perhaps by those whose social status barred them from achieving full recognition) or by *scribae*, rather than the proposing magistrate, since their style is technical and generally pedantic.[34] Subsequent laws repealed earlier ones either explicitly or insofar as they were inconsistent.[35] Convention led to the general observation of such laws as that of the Twelve Tables forbidding legislation aimed at individuals, or the Caecilian Didian Act of 98 BC which forbade adding irrelevancies.[36] Further, Cicero tells us that a law might finish with a clause that if anything illegal be proposed, it was to be deemed not proposed.[37]

RESOLUTIONS OF THE SENATE

All three of our lists include resolutions of the Senate as sources of law. Again, there are different implications. For Cicero the Senate's authority was ideally the strongest force in the constitution, and so account must be taken of its resolutions, even although they were not specific in matters of private law. (It is also worth remembering that magistrates took their proposals for legislation before the Senate for discussion and debate.)[38] For Gaius resolutions of the Senate had replaced assembly legislation; they could directly make new law, 'although this had been questioned'.[39] For Justinian they were yet another historic source, but also – as with Gaius – of legislation in the full sense, which remained in force unless repealed. Just as the Senate for a while took over the function of the assemblies in electing magistrates so, a little later, it had taken over the legislative role. Resolutions of the Senate had been, even in the Republic, in effect binding upon the magistrate – normally the consuls – to whom they were addressed. However, then and in the Principate, the great majority of SCC were administrative; while a significant number deal with criminal law and procedure, relatively few are concerned with private law. SCC were regularly deposited in the *aerarium*, and Cicero tells us that there might be annual volumes.[40] Insofar as they were published, they presumably influenced those who knew of them.

There is argument about when resolutions of the Senate first became binding *per se* without being put into effect by a particular magistrate. This argument is largely artificial, because even a statute needs to be enforced by somebody, or drawn to the attention of a court. Well before the end of the Republic the distinction between *ius civile*, created by *lex* and interpretation, and *ius honorarium*, enforced by a magistrate, was already blurred. Gaius tells us of the Praetor in his Edict putting into effect the *lex Papia Poppaea*;[41] similarly we find the Praetor rejecting the opening of a will of someone who had been murdered before his slaves had been investigated in accordance with the SC *Silanianum*.[42] Moreover, the Senate in the Empire was council to the emperor in succession to the consuls and so imperial acceptance, even without being explicit, gave SCC implicit force because the authority of the emperor was pervasive. Nevertheless, it is clear that the Senate did sometimes during the first century AD issue general rules on matters which would earlier have been dealt with by the assemblies or the magistrates.[43] It seems unlikely, however, at least before the Severi, that the Senate's role was simply and solely to formulate what the emperor wished put into effect, without some input from its members.[44] Certainly the imperial *oratio* could be read – usually by a quaestor – to the Senate and be sure of confirmation. For example:

> For a speech of the deified Hadrian went thus: 'You must decide, conscript fathers, whether it is more equitable that the possessor should not make a profit but pass on the price which he received for another's property, on the ground that the money from the sale of the thing belonging to the inheritance takes the place of the thing itself and so in a way becomes part of the inheritance.' The possessor should therefore make over to the claimant to the inheritance both the thing and any profit from its sale.[45]

The jurists might cite the *oratio* rather than the SC itself, but then one of their number had probably been responsible for drafting it from Hadrian's time onward; only under Severus does a SC read like an imperial edict:

> Tutors and curators are forbidden by an *oratio* of the Emperor Severus to alienate rural or suburban lands. This speech was read in the Senate [in AD 195] and its words are as follows: 'Furthermore, conscript fathers, I forbid tutors and curators to alienate rural or suburban lands, unless . . . '.[46]

Cicero referred to the Senate's resolutions as sources of law because they gave authority to act to magistrates, such as to himself to deal with the Catilinarians, but they were still very different from *lex*. In Gaius' time they had in effect replaced *lex*, although so also had imperial enactments, which were to become the sole source of law not long after. For Justinian, SCC were almost as distant a source of direct legislation as the assembly statutes, but for the same reasons they remained binding unless repealed. And for the same reasons as with legislation in the technical sense, our knowledge of SCC in the field of private law is probably reasonably reliable. Senatorial legislation comes from a much better documented period than the Republic before Cicero. However, the ease with which a SC could be passed, compared with a *lex*, probably meant that many resolutions (of which we may have no record) were concerned with points of detail.

IMPERIAL ENACTMENTS

Imperial enactments (*constitutiones*) naturally did not appear in Cicero's list. For Justinian they were the only living source of law; nothing could have the force of law unless it was according to the emperor's will – which, of course, could be passive in the case of comitial legislation or SCC, which he permitted to remain in force. For Gaius, they must have been the dominant source, but SCC were still being issued. He may well have remembered when the Edict of the Urban Praetor had been finally consolidated under Hadrian (around AD 130 or so).[47] And the work of the jurists was in full flood in his day. Gaius tells us that an imperial enactment covered what the emperor laid down in a judgment (*decretum*), in an edict of general force, or in a rescript, that is a letter (whether from the *ab epistulis* or the *a libellis*) replying to a question of law put to him; the other categories of imperial lawmaking of which we hear were mandates (which were administrative orders), charters to municipalities, grants of individual privileges, and even oral declarations.[48]

Edicts were usually general legislation, wider in scope than the edicts of Republican magistrates, because the emperor's sphere of office was without limit; moreover, they remained valid in perpetuity, even if their author suffered *damnatio memoriae*.[49] We have, for example, the edict of Augustus restricting the torture of household slaves:

> I hold that torture ought not to be applied inevitably to all cases and people, but, when there are capital or rather shocking crimes that cannot be investigated and solved other than by the torture of the slaves, I think it is very efficacious for discovering the truth, and should be used.[50]

Other examples are Claudius' grant of freedom (but freedom as a Junian Latin, not a citizen) to slaves abandoned by their owners because of sickness, or Vespasian's grant of privileges – immunity from compulsory billeting and paying tribute – to physicians as well as teachers of grammar and rhetoric in the cities of the Empire.[51] Edicts, like mandates, were more commonly issued in the spheres of criminal or administrative rather than private law. Mandates might instruct governors to clear their provinces of evil men, or order irenarchs to observe due procedures before remitting accused persons to the governor;[52] they could also directly affect private rights, such as the capacity to marry of someone serving in his home province.[53]

The famous decision of Marcus Aurelius that self-help could amount to violence (*vis*) was in a judgment.

> If creditors proceed against their debtors they should demand what they think due to them through the court; otherwise if they intromit on the property of the debtor without that being granted, the deified Marcus laid down in a judgment that they lost their right as creditor. The words of the judgment are as follows: 'It is best that, if you think you have some claims, you should use due process; in the meantime the other party ought to remain in possession, for you are the claimant.' When Marcian said 'I have used no violence', the emperor said: 'Do you think there is only violence when men are wounded? Violence is when anyone who thinks something is due to him seizes it other than through the court. And I do not think it accords with your honour or dignity or character to do something illegally. Anyone therefore who shall be proved to me to have rashly taken any undelivered property of his debtor without the intervention of the court, shall lose his right as a creditor to what he has alleged is due to him.'[54]

The emperor's judicial decisions might be on first instance or on appeal; they were not necessarily made in formal surroundings, as was true, for example, of Pliny's stint as imperial assessor to Trajan at Centum Cellae.[55] He would normally have the advice of a council; there has been dispute whether the council was general, even if its composition gradually was formalized, or a formal judicial body quite distinct from his 'privy' council, but the latter argument seems deduced from Kunkel's theories of the role of Republican magistrates' councils.[56] It seems right to view these decisions as a sort of case law, but it was very cautious; although a note of the case – taken down probably by shorthand writers – was normally preserved in his office by the *a commentariis*, this report was not really in the public domain. Even if the records were available in the archives, they were presumably filed chronologically, and they were certainly not as a class a ready source for juristic comment, although Paul made two collections of noteworthy cases.[57]

Rescripts were, as the word suggests, written answers by the emperor. Those collected in Justinian's Code were mostly appeals on points of law before a case was actually heard, but rescripts could deal with a whole range of concerns, not necessarily legal at all. Some letters were not technically rescripts, but sent on the emperor's own initiative, although probably in response to some sort of request or inquiry. As a general rule, formal letters were sent from the office of the *ab epistulis* in reply to officials; the best known examples are those sent to Pliny when he was governor of Bithynia by the Emperor Trajan.[58] To private persons the emperor only put his signature (*subscriptio*) to the brief reply appended by the office of the *a libellis* to a copy of the original document; this, or a copy, was then sent to the petitioner.[59] Most of the rescripts we have were probably of this nature: 'Those who keep a wife taken in the act of adultery are guilty of the crime of *lenocinium*, not those who merely have suspicions.'[60]

Rescripts were even less suitable than *decreta* as authoritative statements of the law, because they were normally dependent on the truth of the facts alleged by the party seeking an imperial ruling; judges too, particularly provincial governors, could ask for direction on a point of law, but again the facts were not verifiable by the emperor.[61] Sometimes, however, they had a general character almost like an edict, as with Antoninus Pius' restriction on owners' ill-treatment of their slaves, or his order that accused persons should not be imprisoned if they could find sureties unless the charge was extremely grave.[62] Rescripts seem to have become much more common from Hadrian's time on. This may be partly the accident of survival or the choice of editors, but it is also likely to be a consequence of the consolidation of the Praetor's Edict; moreover, many were sent to the provinces, where juristic advice was unlikely to be available. A rescript could be negative, like Hadrian's reply that the facts of the case would decide whether or not a charge of kidnapping was competent; however, he went on to say that the man was not rightly seen as a kidnapper on whose property one or two runaway slaves were found who had hired themselves out for their keep, as they had done previously.[63] Other rescripts might simply state what had long been accepted as law, such as the right of a bona fide possessor of a slave to acquire through such a slave.[64] Rescripts were clearly filed, like *decreta*, but the jurists of the classical period were not much interested in commenting on them as a whole; we do, however, hear of a collection of Marcus Aurelius' rescripts, entitled *semestria*, and Papirius Justus produced twenty books of *constitutiones* of the *divi fratres* and Marcus Aurelius alone.[65]

In classical law, roughly the law of the Principate, legislation (in the general sense) was largely imperial; statutes passed by the assemblies were instigated by the emperor, and he initiated or approved SCC. From the very start of the Empire (with such enactments as Augustus' edicts for Cyrene)[66] it was clear that imperial pronouncements would be treated as binding, but a satisfactory theoretical basis was lacking.[67] However, power can be said to have created constitutionality; a revolutionary government in the modern world gets legitimated by recognition of the *de facto* situation. Nevertheless, it took two centuries before imperial enactments really supplanted statutes or resolutions of the Senate. The jurisdiction of the Praetor, and then of the Urban Prefect, quite apart from those of other magistrates or officials, continued to be normal for the vast majority of cases; the emperor could settle disputed issues, but nevertheless it is clear that often he did not.[68] Most emperors of the Principate seem to have been responsible for very little active legal development, but then government rather than law reform was their business; this has also been linked to the conservatism of juristic thinking.[69] Whether this really began to change in the fourth century, which is what might be deduced from Justinian's Code, depends partly on the selection made for that code; it may also be due to the cessation of juristic writing.

For Justinian, and indeed during all the Dominate (in legal history the period after Diocletian) the only living source of law was imperial legislation. Nor did it matter what form this took, although we find some new, if rather vague, terms used, such as pragmatic sanction;[70] any imperial pronouncement had the force of law. The Theodosian Code deliberately did not go back to the pre-Constantinian pagan empire – perhaps because it was pagan, perhaps because of the work of Gregory and Hermogenianus. It differed too from these codes in that its compilers were instructed to limit themselves to general laws and laws expressed as edicts.[71]

Further, while the language of the classical jurists and the draftsmen in the imperial offices had normally been severe and factual, particularly in rescripts addressed to individual citizens, the fashionable rhetoric now invaded the process of legislation; one of Justinian's classicizing tendencies was the use of a somewhat simpler style and the cutting back of some of the flourishes of the Theodosian Code. The emperor was glorified by the use of high language, and the actual content of legislation may be difficult to grasp, or to implement; perhaps draftsmen for whom Latin was not their first language may have been less aware of the ambiguities. We find, for example:[72]

> When a man 'marries' in the manner of a woman, a 'woman' about to renounce men, what does he wish, when sex has lost its significance; when the crime is one which it is not profitable to know; when Venus is changed into another form; when love is sought and not found? We order the statutes to arise, the laws to be armed with an avenging sword, that those infamous persons who are now, or who hereafter may be, guilty may be subjected to exquisite punishment.

Or again:

> Many persons who dare to disturb the elements by magic arts do not hesitate to jeopardize the lives of innocent persons and dare to torment them by summoning the spirits of the dead, so that everyone may destroy his enemies by evil arts. A deadly curse shall annihilate such persons (*feralis pestis absumat*), since they are foreign to nature.

Latin continued to be generally used, even in the eastern half of the Empire, into Justinian's time. At Beirut where, as Libanius tells us, young men ambitious of an official or forensic career came to qualify, the texts that formed the basis of legal education were all in Latin, though presumably the lectures were not.[73]

Rescripts seem to have continued to be issued, at least to judges submitting *consultationes*, but, without the jurists to preserve coherence, they were seen as potentially dangerous, disruptive, inconsistent. Hence, as we have mentioned, there was legislation forbidding the use of rescripts as authority.[74] Justinian, on the other hand, was at one stage prepared to take imperial judgments as precedents, although he seems to have changed his mind.[75] It is not surprising then that rescripts were excluded from the Theodosian Code and appear only rarely for the Christian period within Justinian's Code, although that of course included many second and third century rescripts.[76] What does appear – but this may be in part due to the changed nature of that imperial law-making which has been preserved – is that the Later Empire was a period of much more active legislation by the emperors, even if much was reactive to current crises. A notorious example is the continued attempts to control the curial class and keep them working for society that we find in the Theodosian Code.[77] Justinian himself had a vision of changing society through legal policy; he was a thorough-going reformer, not just a tinkerer.[78]

EDICTS OF THE MAGISTRATES

Edicts of the magistrates were, of course, a Republican source of law, and appear in all three lists. Issuing an edict for matters within his sphere of office was an innate magistral power, exercised by censors, consuls, praetors, and aediles, and indeed others. An edict had authority where the magistrate did, but for legal purposes the edict, *the* Edict, was that of the Urban Praetor, whose office had been created in 367 BC precisely for the exercise of jurisdiction. Linked was the edict of his colleague, the Peregrine Praetor, created in 242 BC to exercise jurisdiction among the foreigners in Rome – who were therefore clearly already accepted as capable of using Roman law, or much of it. The Praetor's Edict was known as perpetual, because it was not issued for a specific occasion but intended to be valid throughout his term of office. The first commentary on the Edict was that of Servius Sulpicius Rufus (consul in 51 BC), so it must have already become fairly standard by then, as each Praetor incorporated the bulk of his predecessor's Edict into his own.

As early as the mid-third century BC not only was there the ancient Roman law that was available only to citizens, the *ius civile*, but also Roman law that was recognized as the sort of thing needed by everyone, the *ius gentium*. Into the former category fell family matters such as marriage and the law of succession, formal conveyances – necessary for the alienation of land and of slaves among other things – and usucapion,[79] and certain precise words of contract, deeply rooted in the past (and no longer essential). In the latter category were such matters as the effect of simple delivery to pass ownership of most moveable property, enforceable stipulations,[80] and the legal concepts of sale and hire. Because in many ways the future development of Roman law lay in the *ius gentium*, some have thought that the Peregrine Praetor's edict must have been the key, but we do not know what was in his edict, and surely we should, had it been the creative one. It seems more likely that the Urban Praetor first realized that there was need to give foreigners access to the law – the oldest fiction in the forms of action (offering legal remedies)[81] seems to be 'if he were a citizen' – and that his Edict led the way. The Peregrine Praetor's edict may well have offered many of the same remedies as that of his senior colleague but, rather than adding anything, omitting all that was available only to Roman citizens. Such a general coincidence was implied when Cicero said that he was going to model his provincial edict in Cilicia on the edicts of the praetors at Rome,[82] and is the more likely in that the two offices could, we know, be held by the same man.[83]

Anyway, the Praetor's Edict functioned by offering remedies:

If anyone should be summoned to court by whoever has jurisdiction in some town or village and does not go, or if anyone should summon someone whom he ought not to according to the edict, I shall give an action. . . . I shall give effect to agreements which are without *dolus* and not illegal nor fraudulent. . . . Persons who may not appear in court: those under 17, the completely deaf; if they do not have an advocate, I shall appoint one. . . . What has been done because of threats, I shall not ratify. . . . Unless shipmasters, inn-keepers and stable keepers restore what they have received for safe-keeping, I shall grant an action against them. . . . If someone claims property he has with good title but has not yet usucaped, I shall grant him an action. . . .

Insofar as someone alleges he has made a loan of some thing, I shall grant him an action. . . . For what has been deposited, and not because of tumult, fire, earthquake or shipwreck, I shall grant an action for the simple value, but in these other cases for double damages. . . . How the dowry may be claimed on the dissolution of a marriage. . . . If a widow is alleged to be pregnant, I shall order the unborn child to be put in possession of the estate together with the existing children. . . . When loss has been caused or something is alleged to be missing because of someone's dolose behaviour in a riot, I shall grant double damages against him for a year, after that simple damages. . . . I shall grant an action against someone who, contrary to good morals, has flogged another's slave or had him put to the question without his owner's order. . . .

The Praetor offered a remedy if a case was made; he did not sit as a judge and try the facts. But by his readiness to offer remedies he could, and did, make new law.

The Praetor's function was described as to aid, to supplement, and to correct the *ius civile*,[84] that is the law based on the Twelve Tables and their interpretation. How he did this was described as *ius honorarium* – praetorian law – because it sprang from his office or *honos*. *Ius civile* and *ius honorarium* inevitably blended together in practice, and this blend could interpret the *ius civile* (in the restricted to citizens sense) or the *ius gentium*. But the Praetor did change the law, even by his aiding and supplementing before he ever came to correct. The whole creative period of praetorian law-making seems to have fallen in the period between the *lex Aebutia*, of *c.* 125 BC, and the *leges Iuliae iudiciorum* of Augustus in 17 BC.[85] Before that he essentially administered the law, as advised by the jurists; after that, innovation came from sources closer to the emperor. By the later second century BC at the latest, his powers also included the denial of a remedy to someone who had, on the face of it, a right, such as a freedman suing his patron, or someone pursuing a gambling debt. He could aid the traditional *ius civile*, for instance, by granting actions for developing contracts such as deposit or loan for use,[86] or by granting an interdict (*quorum bonorum*) to enable an heir to take possession of the goods in the estate he was inheriting. He could supplement the *ius civile*, for instance, by granting a policy action (*actio utilis*) on the *lex*

Aquilia where the loss had been caused by omission, or by accepting as a valid will a document with the seals of seven witnesses,[87] even if there was no proof of the formal mancipation of the estate required by the *ius civile* will. His major corrections of the *ius civile* were the introduction of what is commonly called bonitary ownership and of his own rules of intestate succession. These will be explained in an appendix at the end of this chapter.

However, the coming of the Empire brought a diminution in the active powers of the Praetor. Augustus gave jurisdiction over the newly recognized *fideicommissa* (trusts) to the consuls, not the Praetor, and later special praetors exercised this office. Similarly the appointment of tutors was taken from the Urban Praetor and tribunes and given to the consuls or a special praetor. We know of very few new clauses introduced into the Edict in the Empire, and only one by Julian when he consolidated it.[88] Moreover, Julian did not take advantage of the consolidation to systematize the Edict. There is no evidence of this being seen as desirable by either emperor or jurist; but indeed, it would have been somewhat impracticable, since all the commentaries would have become much harder to use had there been a change to the conventional arrangement on which they were based. Thereafter the Edict, and also the other jurisdictional edicts,[89] seems to have remained static; edicts as subordinate legislation could still be issued by functionaries, including provincial governors.

THE JURISTS

The most influential of all the sources of law in the later Republic and the Principate was singular for its lack of formal authority. In the early Republic the college of pontiffs had appointed one of their number each year to 'be in charge of private matters' – to interpret private law.[90] Until 300 BC the pontiffs were always patricians, and they continued to be drawn from the highest ranks in society. Being a pontiff was not incompatible with membership of the Senate and holding high office, including the consulship (which is why it is better not to translate the term as priest). The interpretation of a man of such status would readily be accepted as binding on whoever consulted him, whether magistrates or private citizens. Further, if he chose to interpret *lex* in a particular way, and provided he could convince his colleagues,[91] the new interpretation would change the meaning of the law, would in other words make law. For example, there was a provision in the Twelve Tables which said that a father lost his right to paternal power if he sold his son – as a slave – three times; by interpretation, deliberate release from paternal power (emancipation) was brought about by three sales to a friend, who immediately freed the son each time. Certainly one must describe as making new law the deduction, at some later time, that only one sale was necessary for the emancipation of a daughter or grandchild; another instance is the reasoning by analogy which led to deciding where the guardianship of freed persons lay:

> By the same law of the Twelve Tables the tutory of freed-women and freedmen under puberty goes to the patrons and their children. This tutory is called statutory, not because it was expressly laid down by them for this tutory, but because it has been accepted by interpretation as if it had been intro-duced by the words of the statute. For, by reason that the statute ordered that the estates of freed men and women who died intestate should go to the patrons and their children, the early jurists deemed that the statute willed that tutories also should go to them, because it had ordered that agnates who were heirs should also be tutors.[92]

The pontifical monopoly of interpretation at some stage, whether before or after these developments, disappeared. There may well have been a connection with the fact that Tiberius Coruncanius (who in 254 BC became the first plebeian *pontifex maximus*) first began to teach the law;[93] suitable men, who were not however pontiffs, could thereafter learn the mysteries of interpretation.

The jurists (*iuris consulti, iuris prudentes*) of whom we hear in the ensuing Republican period (from the mid-third century BC) were nearly all members of the Senate – the 300 top men of the state – rich men, powerful men, men of prestige, many of them consuls.[94] By the beginning of the first century BC we have some of their work surviving, in particular from Q.Mucius Scaevola, *pontifex maximus* and consul in 95 BC; among his pupils was C.Aquilius Gallus, praetor in 66 BC, and among his, Servius Sulpicius Rufus, consul in 51.[95] (This sense of 'pupil' implies a personal relationship, rather than sitting in a class, more like a modern doctoral student and his supervisor; the young man might live with his master, and he would follow him about his daily business.[96] Not until the post-classical period do we get law schools.) Mucius was responsible for the *praesumptio Muciana*, the (rebuttable) presumption that her husband had given to her all that a married woman had; Aquilius was responsible for the novatory *stipulatio Aquiliana* which allowed all sorts of debts to be formally discharged; Servius was probably responsible for that *actio Serviana* which gave acquisition of a bankrupt's property.[97] The views of jurists were expressed in legal writings as much as through court practice or the giving of opinions, for example, the fragments of Q.Mucius' eighteen books on the *ius civile*. One of Servius' pupils was A.Ofilius, who wrote the first full commentary on the Praetor's Edict; he was a friend of Julius Caesar, but remained a member of the equestrian order. The jurists of the later Republic were active and inventive; it is they who were almost certainly responsible for nearly all the major changes brought about by the Edict.

We know from Cicero[98] that a jurist must be skilled *ad respondendum et ad agendum et ad cavendum. Ad cavendum* meant drawing up contracts, wills, etc.,[99] while *ad agendum* meant help in litigation, in particular in drafting the formula,[100] and also presumably briefing the orator(s) who would act as advocates. The most important, however, was *ad respondendum,* giving opinions on points of law, perhaps with a view to litigation, perhaps not. Giving such advice was seen by the jurists as a public duty, one that might gain them votes, or repay favours, as well as adding to their dignity, their public name.[101] A Praetor drawing up his Edict, or considering whether to grant a formula in a particular case, might consult a jurist,[102] normally a fellow senator, but so might someone acting as *iudex,* or an advocate, or any private citizen,[103] even a humble one – who presumably would be able to get an introduction from the man whose client he was, or the patron of his municipality, or someone like that. Some opinions seem to have been artificial, in that they were the fruit of hypothetical discussion,[104] but they were no less influential. Others may have had their origins in practice, but were absorbed into legal writings on various topics. These legal opinions were clearly weighty, but they can never have been seen as individually binding, for different jurists gave different advice, for instance, as to the age at which a horse was classed as *res mancipi* and needed formal conveyance.[105] Moreover, no juristic opinion is cited by other jurists as being of authority because it was given by one having the *ius respondendi.* A typical example, also showing the fondness for citing juristic predecessors, is from Paul, who says 'Labeo reports that Trebatius had given an opinion that you can leave a legacy of a field which you may not alienate, but Priscus Fulcinius correctly said this was wrong.'[106] This freedom to disagree persisted until the end of the classical period and beyond, even under Diocletian, but many times a *communis opinio* was reached, whether by accepting the pre-eminent authority of a particular jurist's view or by an imperial enactment,[107] or perhaps even by an adjustment to the Edict.

As the Empire developed, the jurists came to be more closely related to the emperor; they continued to carry weight as individuals through recognition by their fellows and by their status,[108] but this status was itself now increasingly linked to the imperial service. Not all at once, but as time went by, the Praetor's Edict ceased to be a means of juristic development, and new procedures, known as *cognitio*, increasingly with professional judges, arose beside and gradually replaced the formulary system; opportunities for the jurists became more tied to legislation, whether by Senate or emperor, or to the functioning of the imperial administration. In the earlier Principate, roughly from Tiberius to Hadrian, the jurists seem to have continued to hold the highest offices, including the Urban Prefecture, and in particular, although not invariably, the consulship.[109] Then for a while we know less about their careers, or else perhaps they did not hold high office, although Maecian held the (equestrian) prefecture of Egypt under Pius or the *divi fratres* and was on their council,[110] and Cervidius Scaevola was *praefectus vigilum* under Marcus Aurelius. The probable teachers, Pomponius and Gaius, fall into this period. Under Severus and his successors jurists were more likely to be civil servants; Papinian was *a libellis* and later Praetorian Prefect, Paul *a memoria* and (probably) Praetorian Prefect, Ulpian probably *a libellis*, certainly *praefectus annonae*, and later Praetorian Prefect.

However, all through this period the jurists wrote as men having authority in themselves, something apart from the posts they held or the favour they enjoyed. Some of what was written was clearly derived from official experience, but much was simply the further development and polishing of Republican jurisprudence; there was relatively little that was original or innovative.[111] For example:

> We say that a person possesses by stealth who has entered furtively into possession without the knowledge of him who, he suspects, would oppose his taking, and he is fearful that

this would happen. On the other hand, a person, not in possession by stealth, who has concealed himself is not in such a case that he should be held to possess by stealth; for the factor to be considered is not the manner of holding possession but its original acquisition; and no one acquires possession by stealth who acquires possession with the knowledge or consent of the thing's owner, or on any ground of good faith. Pomponius accordingly says that a person acquires possession by stealth who enters furtively into possession, fearing opposition and without the knowledge of the man of whom he is apprehensive. Suppose a man to go to market without leaving someone behind and, while he is returning from the market, someone seizes possession; Labeo says that this person possesses by stealth, and so the man who went to market remains in [technical] possession; but if the intruder does not admit the owner on his return, he is regarded as possessing by force rather than by stealth.[112]

There also appeared textbooks for beginners, of which the best example is Gaius' Institutes (or Institutions), and textbooks at a more advanced level, called *regulae, definitiones,* or *sententiae.*[113] Of these the best known example, although put together post-classically, probably in the late third century, is *Pauli Sententiae,* the *Opinions* of Paul. These kinds of writing contained dogmatic statements of the law; the latter class also included collections of maxims, and might deal with criminal law. For example, Gaius introduced his exposition of the four consensual contracts:

Obligations are created by consent in buying and selling, letting and hiring, partnership, and mandate. We say that obligations are contracted by consent in these cases because there is no requirement of either [spoken] words or writing, but it is sufficient that the parties have consented. And so such contracts may be made between absent parties, for instance by letter or by messenger; when, quite otherwise, an oral obligation is not possible between absent parties. Further, in these contracts one party is obliged to the other on the same account as the other is to the one for what ought to be done in good faith and justice; when, quite otherwise, in oral obligations the one party stipulates and the other promises, and in written contracts the one imposes the obligation and the other is obligated.[114]

Gaius then goes on to deal in more detail with each of the four. Paul explains the consequence of animals causing loss:[115]

> 1. If a four-legged animal causes loss or does damage or consumes something, an action is given against its owner for him either to pay the cost of the loss or to surrender the animal; and this is also laid down for a dog by the *lex Pesolania*. 1a. If anyone keeping a fierce dog in a courtyard or on the public streets during daylight hours does not restrain him on a lead, any loss incurred is to be paid for by the owner. 1b. If anyone permits a horse or other animal having the mange to move about in such a way that it becomes mixed up in the herds or flocks of a neighbour and infects them with its own sickness, the owner is similarly to make amends for any loss incurred through it. 2. The praetor forbids wild animals to be held together in a place which is a public path; and so, whether loss is incurred through its own action or because it has caused one person to harm another, an extra-ordinary action, in proportion to the offence, is given against the owner or keeper, particularly if someone was killed because of this. 3. If someone by his own incitement provokes a wild beast or some other four-legged animal into attacking him and loss is incurred, no action is given against the owner or keeper. 4. Against travellers, who carry snakes about and produce them, an action will be given in proportion to the offence if loss is incurred by anyone through fear of them.

Legal traditionalism is apparent in the fact that, even in the third century, jurists such as Ulpian and Paul wrote separate treatises on the old *ius civile* of the Twelve Tables and their interpretation (often entitled, as with these two authors, *ad Sabinum*) and on the *ius honorarium – ad edictum*. However, the latter class often incorporated the relevant areas of the *ius civile* into the treatment of praetorian law. Treatises on the law as a whole were usually called *digesta*, such as those of Celsus and Julian, but where they were casuistic in approach they might be called *disputationes* (e.g. Tryphoninus'), *quaestiones* (e.g. Africanus'), *responsa* (e.g. Papinian's). There were commentaries on particular laws, such as Gaius on the Twelve Tables, Mauricianus on the *lex Julia et Papia*, Marcian on the SC *Turpillianum*; there were also some monographs on particular areas of law, such as Paul on dowry, Papinian on adultery, Pomponius on trusts. Then there were works on public law, such as Ulpian on the duties of a provincial governor, Callistratus on the law of the fisc, Macer on criminal courts. Perhaps not surprisingly, it was in this last area that the late classical jurists were most original in their writings, although the disappearance of the *quaestiones perpetuae*, the standing jury courts introduced in the late Republic, made more difficult a systematic approach to criminal law.[116] Modestinus, the last of the great jurists, was a pupil of Ulpian; he held the office of prefect of the night watch.[117] He was the only jurist to write a work – *de excusationibus*, on excuses from tutory and other public burdens – in Greek, doubtless to cater for the new mass of citizens created by Caracalla's Edict of 212, but it was an unconscious prophecy of things to come, of the shift in the balance of power within the Empire to Constantinople. From the reign of Constantine on there are many lawyers, but no more jurists in the traditional sense,[118] only legal advisers in the imperial service, law professors in the schools, and advocates and judges in the courts.[119] As an individual source of law jurisprudence was dead.

Appendix on praetorian lawmaking

In classical law certain property (Italic land, rustic praedial servitudes, slaves, and beasts of draught and burden) needed formal conveyance (*mancipatio* or *in iure cessio*) for title to pass under the civil law; if such property was conveyed informally by the original owner (O), the acquirer (A) who possessed it in good faith and on good grounds (*iusta causa*) could go on to usucape (acquire by continuing to possess) moveables in one year, land in two. If a third party (T) took it from A during this period, A could normally recover by interdict; if T challenged A, A could in theory prove O's delivery, and anyway he was already in possession. O could not vindicate (claim the property as his) from A because he would be met by the defence of bad faith (*dolus*) since he had delivered it. Where the real innovation came was in the case that somehow the property came into the possession of O, before the period of usucapion had been completed. A could not claim it as technically his own because he did not (yet) have title; however, the Praetor granted A an action against O (or *a fortiori* against T) with the fiction that the usucapion period had been completed (*actio Publiciana*). In this way formal conveyance ceased to be strictly necessary, although, of course, it was psychologically safer.

Under the law of the Twelve Tables, if a man died intestate

(without making a will or leaving only an invalid one) his heirs were, first, his children – and possibly other direct descendants – (*sui heredes*), then his nearest agnate – relations in the nearest degree through the male line, as with our surname system – and then his clan or members of it. The Praetor preferred to give possession of the deceased's estate (*bonorum possessio*) – not the 'inheritance' (*hereditas*) as such because that was governed by the *ius civile* – to blood relations through the female line or, failing them, to the widow, rather than to the clan, an obsolescent institution by the end of the Republic. Eventually the Praetor came to give possession of the estate to someone named in a will which satisfied his criteria, and denied the inheritance to the intestate civil law heir.

NOTES

1 Cited in ELH, 2.9.6.

2 Cicero, *Topica* 5.28.

3 G. 1.1–7.

4 *Inst.* 1.2. The text of Papinian in D 1.1.7 and the other introductory fragments in the first title are not independent; they may be classical, but they were edited by Justinian.

5 Crook (1967), at p. 27.

6 See D 3.5.20*pr.*, Paul 9 *ad ed*, citing Servius, and 44.1.14, Alfenus 2 *dig*; both are concerned with the Praetor's decretal remedies, supplementing the *ius civile*; cf. Q.Mucius' views on partnership shares – G 3.149. In the Principate see, for example, the rescript of Antoninus Pius cited in D 4.1.7*pr.*, Marcellus 3 *dig.*

7 D 1.1.1*pr.*, Ulpian 1 *inst.*

8 *Inst.* 1.1.*pr.* (= D 1.1.10*pr.*, Ulpian 1 *reg.*)

9 E.g. D 1.3.34, Ulpian 4 *de off.proconsulis*; cf. CJ 8.52.1, AD 224, which seems to refer to a sort of *ius commune.*

10 See Schiller (1978), p. 264ff, citing P.Oxy. II 237.VII.12–16 of AD 186, and P.Oxy. VI.899.24–32, of AD 200, and referring to FIRA i 85.

11 D 1.4.1.2, Ulpian 1 *inst.*

12 E.g. Pliny's doubts about how to handle the Christians – *Ep.* 10.96–7.

13 E.g. CTh 1.2.2, AD 315; CTh 1.2.11, AD 398; CJ 1.14.3, AD 426.

14 Cf. CJ 1.14.12 with 7.45.13.

15 D 9.2.2.2, Gaius 7 *ad ed.prov.* Sheep, goats, cattle, horses, mules and asses were classified as *pecudes*, and so were pigs after some debate; dogs were clearly not. Elephants and camels had the right characteristics, and ought to be, but they had not been known to custom when the law was passed.

16 Watson (1974a), 170–1, argues that custom cannot have been created by the jurists; agreed, but their recognition led to its acceptance.

17 In Julian's famous text (D 1.3.32.1, 84 *dig*) on the force of custom,

and of desuetude, one could well replace 'the people' with 'the jurists'; see also Thomas (1963).

18   D 18.6.1.4, Ulpian 28 *ad Sab* – 'per corbem'.

19   E.g. Pliny *Ep.* 10.108–9 or 112–13.

20   On and off it included Mesopotamia and Armenia.

21   Compare, much later, Bartolus discussing the number of witnesses for a will in Venice – Clarence Smith (1970) at 167ff.

22   D 21.2.6, Gaius 10 *ad ed.prov,* or 26.7.7.10, Ulpian 35 *ad ed.*

23   On the *lex Tullia de ambitu* see, for example, Cicero *pro Murena* 2.3; 3.5; 22.45; 32.67; 41.89.

24   Watson (1974a), p. 15.

25   D 9.2.2*pr.,* Gaius 7 *ad ed.prov.*

26   D 9.2.27.4-5, Ulpian 18 *ad ed.*

27   *Inst.* 4.18; see also Robinson (1991–2).

28   The text of the *lex Irnitana* is published in Gonzalez (1986).

29   Gellius 5.19.9 gives the words of the proposal; cf. G 1.98–102.

30   Livy 3.34.6.

31   E.g. indirect actions (*actiones utiles*) under the *lex Aquilia* – *Inst.* 4.3.16, but perhaps more clearly in *Inst.* 4.6.3 on actions; cf. *Inst.* 4.18*pr.,* on which see Robinson (1991–2), cited above.

32   Watson (1992) *passim.*

33   Cicero *pro Balbo* 8.21; cf. Watson (1974a), 61f.

34   E.g., the *tabula Heracleensis,* often known as the *lex Julia municipalis,* FIRA I 13, = ARS no. 113.

35   XII T 12.5.

36   XII T 9.1; Rotondi (1912), p. 335.

37   Cicero, *pro Caecina* 33.95: 'si quid ius non esset rogarier, eius ea lege nihilum rogatum'.

38   See Nicolet (1958).

39   G 1.4.

40   Cicero *ad Att.* 13.33.3.

41   G 3.50, although it is to be remembered that the law is of the Empire, when the roles of the sources of law were being redefined; cf. G 3.32.

42   D 29.5.3.18, Ulpian, 50 *ad ed*; cf. 16.1.2.1, Ulpian 29 *ad ed,* on the SC Velleanum.

43   E.g. the SC Libonianum on forgery or the SC Neronianum on the validity of certain legacies, or the SC Silanianum which had effect on both the criminal law and the law of succession.

44   Robinson (1996).

45   D 5.3.22, Paul 20 *ad ed.*

46   D 27.9.1*pr.*–2, Ulpian 35 *ad ed.*

47   Recorded in the preliminaries to the Digest, *c. Tanta* 18; see Jolowicz, 356f.

48   For example, for charters, see the *lex municipii Malacitani* – FIRA i 24 = ARS no. 192; for individual privileges, D 1.4.1.2, Ulpian 1 *inst,* and FIRA i 82 = ARS no. 175; for an oral speech, FV 195.

49   D 48.3.2.1, Papinian 1 *de adulteriis.*

50   D 48.18.8*pr.,* Paul 2 *de adulteris.*

51 D 40.8.2, Modestinus 6 *reg*; FIRA i 73 = ARS no. 185; cf. D 27.1.6.2, Modestinus 2 *exc*, for Antoninus Pius on this topic; see also Robinson (1994), pp. 127ff.

52 D 1.18.3, Paul 13 *ad Sab*; 48.3.6.1, Marcian 2 *de iud.pub.*

53 D 23.3.65, Paul 7 *resp.*

54 D 48.7.7, Callistratus 5 *de cogn*; see also 4.4.38*pr.*, Paul 1 *decret*; 28.4.3, Marcellus 29 *dig*; 40.5.38, Paul 3 *decret.*

55 Pliny *Ep.* 6.31; cf. Millar (1967).

56 Crook (1955) vs. Kunkel (1967 & 1968).

57 Schulz (1953), p. 154.

58 Pliny *Ep.* Book 10; the particularity makes them generally classifiable as rescripts rather than *mandata*, although mandates are mentioned in e.g. *Ep.* 10.96. Interestingly, no jurist seems to have made use of Pliny's collection.

59 Williams (1974) argues that there was blanket publication of *subscriptiones*, as least inconvenient for the office of the *a libellis.*

60 CJ 9.9.2, AD 199.

61 CJ 7.61.1, AD 319.

62 G 1.53, cf. *Inst.* 1.8.2; D 48.3.3, Ulpian 7 *de off.proconsulis.*

63 D 48.15.6*pr.*–1, Callistratus 6 *de cogn*; cf. Robinson (1995) 32ff.

64 CJ 3.32.1, AD 210; cf. G 2.86 & 92; see also D 19.2.19.9, Ulpian 32 *ad ed.*

65 See Schulz (1953), p. 153.

66 FIRA i 68 = ARS no. 148.

67 *Lex de imperio Vespasiani* – FIRA i 15, vv.18–21 = ARS no. 183; G 1.5; D 1.1.1.11, Pomponius *enchir*; 1.4.1*pr.*, Ulpian 1 *inst.*

68 For example, the definition of *specificatio* was not settled until Justinian – *Inst.* 2.1.25.

69 Schulz (1953), pp. 128f; but see Gardner (1996).

70 In the preliminaries to Justinian's Code, *c.Summa* s. 4; see also App. 7 to Justinian's Novels. (On the other hand, there was special ink reserved for imperial use – CJ 1.23.6, AD 470.)

71 CTh 1.1.6, AD 435.

72 CTh 9.7.3, AD 342 and 9.16.5, AD 357, both in Pharr's translation.

73 Schulz (1953), pp. 268f.

74 CTh 1.2.2 & 3, AD 315 & 316; 1.2.11, AD 398; CJ 1.14.3, AD 426.

75 CJ 1.14.12, AD 529; *NovJ* 113.1, AD 541.

76 *Nov.* Anthemius 1 (AD 468) shows us a general statement of the law made to a Praetorian Prefect which arose out of the particular petition of one Julia.

77 CTh 12.1.

78 Robinson (1987).

79 Usucapion is the positive acquisition of ownership, through the relevant lapse of time, of property, whether land or moveables, acquired in good faith and with apparent title; see Appendix on praetorian lawmaking at the end of this chapter.

80 A formal question and answer creating a unilateral obligation in the promisor; with the usual reservations about legality and morality, any alienating or giving or doing or abstaining could be promised by stipulation.

81 See ch. 4.

82   Cicero *ad Att.* 6.1.15.

83   Livy 24.44. & 25.3 of 214 & 212 BC, although this was in the exceptional circumstances of the Punic War; see Serrao (1954), p. 22f.

84   D 1.1.7.1, Papinian 2 *definit.*

85   See Kelly (1966b); Watson (1968).

86   G 4.47.

87   Cicero *Verr.*II 1.117 is not clear whether five would have been enough, as representing the witnesses to the mancipation between the testator and the executor.

88   D 37.8.3, Marcellus 9 *dig.* On the fact of the consolidation, see ch. 1.

89   Those of the Peregrine Praetor and the aediles; also presumably the *edictum provinciale* on which Gaius commented, which Buckland (1934) reckoned extended praetorian law to citizens living in the provinces, while governors issued other edicts for the 'natives'.

90   D 1.2.2.6, Pomponius *enchiridion.*

91   Was there the possibility of *intercessio*, or some similar device, among pontiffs?

92   G 1.165.

93   D 1.2.2.6 & 35 & 38, Pomponius *enchiridion*: 'et quidem ex omnibus qui scientiam nancti sunt ante Tiberium Coruncanium publice professum neminem traditur; ceteri autem ad hunc vel in latenti ius civile retinere cogitabant solumque consultatoribus vacare potius quam discere volentibus se praestabant. . . . Tiberius Coruncanius, ut dixi, qui primus profiteri coepit.'

94   See ch. 1.

95   D 1.2.2.43, Pomponius *enchiridion.*

96   Cicero *de or.* 1.43.191; *Brutus* 89.306; cf. Gellius 13.13.1.

97   D 24.1.51, Pomponius 5 *ad Q.Mucium*; 46.4.18, Florentinus 8 *inst*; G 4.34–5. The *formula Rutiliana* also mentioned in this passage of Gaius can probably be ascribed to Rutilius Rufus. Watson (1968) points out that we only know for certain – always through Cicero – the dates of four insertions in the Edict, falling between 118 BC, or just before, and 66 BC.

98   Cicero *de or.* 1.48.212; cf. *Topica* 17.65–6.

99   E.g. Varro *de re r.*2.3.5; D 28.6.39*pr.*, Javolenus 1 *ex post.Lab.* This is known as cautelary jurisprudence.

100   See ch. 4.

101   On this question of favours, see Kelly (1966a), especially ch. 2; Watson (1995), App.C; cf. Cicero *pro Murena* 4.9; *de off.* 2.19.65.

102   E.g. D 4.4.3.1, Ulpian 11 *ad ed*, citing Celsus.

103   Cicero *Topica* 17.65–6; Gellius 14.2; D 31.47, Proculus 6 *ep.* Such advice could even be a duty – 22.6.9.3, Paul *de iuris et facti ignorantia*, citing Labeo.

104   Cicero *Topica* 14.56.

105   Sabinians at birth, Proculians when broken in – G 2.15. On the Schools, see ch. 5. For some other contradictory *responsa*, see Cicero *ad fam.* 7.21–2; D 33.7.16.1, Alfenus 2 *dig. a Paulo epit*; G 3.140.

106   D 31.49.2, Paul 5 *ad l. Iuliam et Papiam*; 'cuius commercium non habes' presumably means the field could not be alienated because people had been buried there.

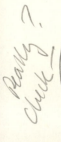
really ?
check

107 E.g. D 2.1.11*pr.*, Gaius 1 *ad ed.prov.* See also Gualandi (1963).
108 The *ius respondendi* was treated in ch. 1. Treatment of individual jurists will be found in Kunkel (1967a), Jolowicz, and Schiller (1978).
109 For example, Julian – ILS 8973 = CIL VIII 24094.
110 D 37.14.17, Ulpian 11 *ad l. Iuliam et Papiam*; see also CIL XIV 5347–8.
111 Schulz (1953), pp. 128f., suggests that they could easily – if they had had the will – have rationalized praetorian estate-possession, and the proprietary capacity of those in paternal power, or produced a generalized contract in writing.
112 D 41.2.6, Ulpian 70 *ad ed*; the Watson translation has been slightly modified; cf. Gordon (1994).
113 See Stein (1966).
114 G 3.135–7.
115 PS 1.15.
116 Robinson (1995), ch. 1.
117 FIRA iii 165 – *lis fullonum*; see also de Robertis (1982).
118 CJ 1.14.1, AD 316.
119 *Nov.* Th 1, AD 438; see Liebs (1987) for the West, and most conveniently still Schulz (1953), pp. 268–77.

Chapter 3

Transmission

INTRODUCTORY

This chapter is concerned with the survival of the legal sources, that is, the material forms which have come to us from antiquity. We discussed the authority for the various sources of law in The Makers of Roman Law (chapter 1) and their form in the Sources chapter (chapter 2); here the angle of approach is where to find them, and to describe briefly their transmission to us. In this context a source of law is anything which gives us in the modern (or medieval or early modern) world information that can be applied to explain law, whether in theory or in practice. It is not the same as the definitions we have previously used, either the constitutional, or the formal – that which might have been used by a Roman who wanted to discover the existing state of his law. This chapter deals with the material which modern romanists use to describe, explain, and discuss the law of the ancient Romans.

This, above all, means the survival of the Justinianic texts, but there are manuscripts containing other juristic work, and many literary references to legislation, resolutions of the Senate, the enactments of emperors, and other matters pertaining to the administration of the law, including specific transactions. Then there are the non-literary survivals. The aim in this chapter is also to enable the student to know who has edited the sources, and where the most recent editions may be found; where it is possible, translations are recommended. It may need stressing that often, when pursuing a particular point, it is worth looking at an edition by Cujas, Gothofredus or some other of the Humanist scholars. Mommsen and the other great German editors of the later nineteenth century did not necessarily come to the best conclusions – and some manuscripts had disappeared by their time; nor should they be expected to have established the texts in perpetuity. Nevertheless, the twentieth century has not seen much in the way of major editions; modern romanists have largely built on the generally accepted work of their nineteenth-century predecessors. How far the legal texts reflect the law of the period in which they purport to have been written is one of the issues discussed in chapter 5.

Apart from Justinian's compilation (known as the *Corpus Iuris Civilis*), and the Theodosian Code, almost all the sources of law in the technical sense are most conveniently and easily found in the collection known as FIRA. FIRA volume i gives texts of legislation,[1] or sources akin to legislation, such as the Praetor's Edict; volume ii contains the surviving jurisprudence from before Justinian's codification. The collection made in FIRA iii of *negotia*, legal transactions between parties, is divided into the law of persons, information on *collegia* (guilds or clubs), wills and testamentary matters, affairs of sacral or public law, records of ownership and possession, servitudes and other real rights, simple debts, consensual contracts, and matters brought to judgment; they show law in practice, the mechanisms of the law, the putting into effect of legislation and interpretation.[2] Obviously such a collection is a selection from what was available when it was put together. Some important finds have been made relatively recently, such as the *lex Irnitana*, or the Herculaneum Tablets, and lesser but still interesting groups of documents such as those from Vindolanda on Hadrian's Wall. Another fundamental collection is the *Textes de droit romain*, edited by P.F.Girard, and revised by F.Senn; its three parts are distributed in the same way as for FIRA.[3] Most of the material in FIRA i and some in iii is translated in *Ancient Roman Statutes*, although it is an independent work and includes some other material. A new collection, entitled *Roman Statutes*, edited by M.H.Crawford, has just been published; its scope is more limited, as the title suggests.

It should be mentioned here that certain sources as described in chapters 1 and 2 have no independent existence in terms of this chapter. The Twelve Tables are merely a construct, from literary as much as legal writings. Most notably there is no independent evidence for the Praetor's Edict, although it seems to have survived in written form into Justinian's time.[4] The Edict was carefully reconstructed by Lenel,[5] but it is drawn from the existing juristic sources in the Digest; his overall picture is accepted, although there have been numerous challenges on detail. The same is true of the edict of the aediles. Also needing to be deduced are the Codes of Gregorius and Hermogenianus.[6] Custom and equity, as we have explained, are also known to us only through the interpretation of the jurists.

The legal sources, in the forms we shall shortly list, are mostly derived from parchment manuscripts (with the occasional supplementary papyrus). So too are the literary and most of the technical sources which tell us about law, or from which deductions may be made as to the law. We have, however, legislation of various kinds preserved not only in literary form but also in inscriptions on stone or bronze; there are many other inscriptions which give us information about personal details of the great and of the humble. Papyri record certain legislative acts, and there are many documents dealing with transactions with a legal content, including court procedures. A fair number of wax tablets survive which record transactions with a legal content. Then there are coins, which can give legal information. Archaeology too can in some contexts inform us about the law; we can visit, for example, the remains of the aqueducts, or read the reports of the excavation of burial sites. It is clear, however, that the bulk of our sources come from manuscripts.

THE LEGAL SOURCES

The principal source for modern romanists is the collection known as the *Corpus Iuris Civilis*, authorized by the Emperor Justinian in the earlier sixth century. That consists of four separate works, the Institutes, the Digest, the Code, and the Novels.[7] Subsidiary sources, but still of immense importance, are, first, the Theodosian Code of the mid-fifth century and, second, a number of legal works – writings by lawyers for other lawyers, for law students, or for persons who must administer the law – which almost all come from the immediately post-classical period, the later third and early fourth centuries. All these juristic works survived independently of Justinian's codification. Of them, the *Institutes* of Gaius are exceptional, in that they were written in the later second century, in the classical period of Roman law. The Theodosian Code is normally published on its own, with the addition of some earlier imperial enactments, known as the Sirmondian Constitutions (Sirmond being their editor and 'constitutio' being the word

generally translated in this book as 'enactment'), and also the
Novels (or new laws) of Theodosius himself and the immediately
succeeding emperors.

The *Corpus Iuris Civilis*

Justinian's collection, which was described briefly in chapter 1, was
well known to the medieval world, primarily as it was transmitted
through the Great Gloss of Accursius;[8] it continued to be used
in this glossed form into the nineteenth century. Haloander
(1501–31) produced a fresh edition, but the first scholarly edition,
using the title *Corpus Iuris Civilis*, and one which remained the
standard edition into the nineteenth century, was that of Dionysius
Gothofredus in 1583.[9] Modern textual criticism then led to the
publication of what is known as the stereotype edition,[10] in three
volumes in double column; this is the most widely used version.
The *Corpus* is nowadays cited by book, title, and fragment or *lex*,
with the first sentence in each fragment being known as *principium*
and the next being s. 1 (rather like the British first floor being
one up). It used, however, to be cited by reference to the titles in
the individual parts (which the medieval lawyers knew by heart)
and to the first words of the fragment therein; for example, *l*[*ex*]
legis Fabiae crimine § *illud non est* D. *de lege Fabia*, or l.3 §1 D. *de lege
Fabia* (48.15), is to us D 48.15.3.1. The enactments which are the
preliminaries to the individual parts, ordering their compilation
and promulgation and so on, are cited as, for the Institutes, *Inst.
c.* (or *const.*) *Imperatoriam Maiestatem*, for the Digest, *D const. Deo
Auctore*, *Omnem*, and *Tanta* (*Dedoken* in its Greek version) and for
the Code, *CJ const. Haec quae necessario*, *Summa*, and *Cordi*. There are
translations into the major European languages of the whole
Corpus Iuris, but most are unsatisfactory.[11]

The Institutes, or Institutions, of Justinian, apart from fragments, is not found in a manuscript earlier than the ninth century,
but there were many from the twelfth century on. The first printed
edition appeared in 1468, but Cujas (1522–90) produced the first
scholarly edition in 1585. However, the discovery of virtually the
complete text of Gaius' Institutes in 1816 led to a considerable
revision, since so much of Justinian was based directly on Gaius.[12]
This culminated in the editions of P. Krüger in 1867 (fourth
edition 1921), which is printed in vol. I of the stereotype *Corpus*,
and Huschke's Teubner edition of 1868. The work is cited usually

as *Inst.* but also as *J.* or *I.*; it is divided into (four) books, titles, and sentences. A recent satisfactory version of the Institutes with an English translation and commentary is that of Thomas.[13]

For the Digest we have an almost contemporaneous – and very clear – manuscript, one from the late sixth or early seventh centuries, which appeared in the eleventh century and was held at Pisa by the twelfth. It has been known as the Florentine ever since it was taken there as loot in 1406; there is a photocopy, itself rare. A few fragments in other manuscripts also survive from before the ninth century. There was another complete manuscript, although it is now lost, and presumably destroyed, termed S[ecundus], itself dating from the late eleventh century, which used another source as well as the Florentine. After the revival of Roman law at Bologna there were many mss using S as well as F; they are known as the Vulgate MSS. Politian (1454–94) was the first man who studied the Florentine in order to correct a printed edition; the Florentine itself was published in 1553. Haloander's edition, although made without access to the Florentine, is notable for how many of his suggestions, preserved in the footnotes to the stereotype Digest, make excellent sense. The most scholarly edition of the Digest is the two-volume *editio maior* by Theodor Mommsen, published in 1870.[14] Another edition, based largely on Mommsen, was produced in Italy in 1931, with an amended edition in 1960.[15] The Digest is cited as D or *Dig*; probably through a plain mistake, the sign *ff* was also long used to indicate the Digest. It is divided into (fifty) books, titles[16] and fragments, and where applicable into sentences within each fragment. The most recent translation of the Digest into English is the version under the general editorship of Alan Watson.[17]

There are some external aids to the reconstruction of the original. The *Basilica*, a Greek compilation completed under Leo the Wise (886–911), put together into one integrated sequence of sixty books the Digest and Code and also abbreviated versions of the Institutes and Novels; moreover, it included writings of jurists contemporary with Justinian, as well as some later legislation.[18] When Humanist jurists again became competent in Greek, they could check readings in the *Corpus* against it, and take account of the juristic comments on the codification. As well as the main Digest manuscript we have, in accordance with Justinian's orders, also an index in Greek to the jurists; this is known as the *Index Florentinus*. There are discrepancies between the Index and the text of the Digest; some works are listed in the Index which are not found in the Digest, and some found which are not listed.[19] Apart from Julian and Papinian, the jurists are listed in approximate chronological order, from Q. Mucius Scaevola to Hermogenianus.

The basic method used for compiling the Digest in a bare three years was grasped by Bluhme in 1818.[20] There have been modifications, but no fundamental challenge, to his work.[21] The compilers under Tribonian first devised a draft scheme of arrangement for the books and titles, on a system which followed the traditional edictal order and then used legislation, whether of the assemblies, the Senate, or the emperors; this scheme had been used by Julian for his *Digesta*, and the title may well have been a compliment to his memory. They then divided the juristic works to be read into four groups, or perhaps three, with the fourth appearing as oversights were remedied. The commission then divided itself into committees for reading each of these three 'masses', the Sabinian, the Edictal, and the Papinianic, concurrently; the Appendix mass was done last. As the works were read, excerpted and edited they were in each group distributed according to the overall scheme. Then they were put together into titles, usually with the extracts from whatever was in the context the largest mass first, but with occasional mingling in of texts from another mass.

The manuscript history of the Code is confused; some enactments were abbreviated, and others omitted where they had been invalidated by Justinian's later legislation. Inscriptions, giving the addressee and date of enactment, were confused with the subscriptions (of the enactments immediately above them), giving the place and date of promulgation. Then, the last three of its original twelve books seem to have been dropped in the eighth or ninth centuries, although recovered in the eleventh. When they were available again, they were normally combined with the Institutes, the *Authenticum* (one version of Justinian's Novels) and the *Libri Feudorum*. Haloander's 1530 edition of the Code contained only books 1 to 9. The Greek enactments were omitted from the western manuscripts or printed editions until Cujas and Agustín restored them later in the sixteenth century; Cujas also edited books 10–12. The complete Code was published by Dionysius Gothofredus in his *Corpus Iuris*. The definitive modern edition of the Code is Paul Krüger's *editio maior* of 1877; it is used for the stereotype, with corrections. The Code is cited as C. or CJ; it is divided into (twelve) books, titles, and *leges* (or imperial enactments), and where applicable into sentences within each. No English translation has been published of the Code alone.

The Code was drawn from the *Codices Gregorianus* and *Hermogenianus* and the Theodosian Code, and also clearly from the imperial archives. Within each title, the order of which mostly follows that of the Theodosian Code, the enactments are arranged in chronological order. It includes rescripts as well as general legislation, the latter mostly from the Dominate. Much of the rhetorical bombast in the language of the Theodosian Code was cut back. Unlike the earlier codes, only legislation that was currently in force was to be included; the Digest provided ample material for the study of dogmatic development in the law schools.

Because never officially collected, the Novels of Justinian have an even more confused history. Those directed to the eastern half of the Empire were in Greek, those to the West in Latin. The *Epitome of Julian* is the name given to the collection of 122 enactments, issued in Greek but translated into Latin, made during Justinian's lifetime; the oldest manuscripts are of the late seventh or early eighth centuries. Because it was linguistically accessible this was long the only edition known in the West. Another Latin collection of 134 Novels was known from the eleventh century, and named the *Authenticum* because it may have been – as Irnerius believed – the version promulgated in Rome after Justinian's reconquest in 554. The third collection, used by the compilers of the Basilica, was of 168 Greek Novels, made after Justinian's death; manuscripts survive from the thirteenth and fourteenth century. Because of the language, this only became accessible to the scholars of the Renaissance, such as Haloander, and Scrymgeour (1506–72). The standard modern edition, to be found in the stereotype, is that of Schöll, completed by Kroll in 1895; Kroll's latest revisions were published in the stereotype in 1928. Outside the stereotype *Corpus*, but held of equal stature, is the edition of the Novels by von Lingenthal. There is no satisfactory English translation. However, the Novels of Justinian are rather part of Byzantine than Roman legal history, and they have had much less influence on later European law than the Institutes, Digest, and Code.

The pre-Justinianic codes[22]

The two codes of Gregorius and Hermogenianus have to be reconstructed from the post-classical juristic writings and from the Germanic codes in which the enactments they contained were included. They gave the actual words of imperial rulings, arranged systematically, that is, the first thirteen books followed the order of the Edict, with a fourteenth on criminal law and two more on public law. The most useful edition is still Krüger's;[23] the FIRA version gives only the Visigothic epitome.[24] Probably all the pre-Constantinian material in Justinian's Code is derived from them. They are more likely to be imperially authorized collections than private enterprise in view of their subsequent use and their inclusion in Justinian's Code. When they were produced, the emperors had for more than a century been the sole active source of law; one can ascribe to Diocletian's classicizing tendencies the use of the compilers' names rather than his own.

The Theodosian Code has also to be reconstructed, although in a less drastic sense. We have much of it as extracted for the *Lex Romana Visigothorum*, with an *interpretatio*. A number of manuscripts have been found containing fragments of the original as it was in force before the disappearance of the western Empire; very considerable sections are still missing. Jacobus Gothofredus (1578–1652), son of Dionysius, was the first to produce a critical edition with a scholarly commentary.[25] The normal modern edition is that edited by Mommsen, published in 1905 with an important introduction of some 300 pages; Krüger had begun an edition, with a different order of titles in the first five fragmentary books. Mommsen's edition includes the Sirmondian Constitutions, sixteen enactments dealing with ecclesiastical law issued prior to the Theodosian code, and various post-Theodosian Novels.[26] There is a fairly good English translation by Clyde Pharr; it faithfully reflects the obscurity of the original.

The Sirmondian collection consists apparently of something close to the original texts; ten of these enactments appear, altered, in the Theodosian Code. The compilers of the Code were specifically ordered to shorten and rearrange their texts,[27] as were Justinian's compilers later. Although they cited the provenance of each enactment, research has shown that these are frequently either false or confused; this is more likely due to the difficulties of discovering authentic texts than carelessness. All enactments subsequent to 312 were made of no validity from 1 January 439, when the Code came into force; this had no effect on the authority of the earlier Codes of Gregory and Hermogenianus. Theodosius II's original plan to combine juristic extracts and earlier legislation in a complete code never came to anything.[28]

Not strictly part of Roman law, but needing to be mentioned briefly here because they have been the path for the transmission of so much of Roman law, are the Germanic codes or collections of the fifth and sixth centuries.[29] The *Edict* of Theodoric was long ascribed to Theodoric, king of the Ostrogoths, and dated to around 500, but strong arguments have been proposed for dating it to around 460 and the Visigothic kingdom in south-western Gaul.[30] It is cited as ET or *EdTheod*, by sentence. The *Lex Romana Burgundionum* dates from the reign of King Gundobad, 474–516.[31] It is cited as LRB by title and sentence. The *Lex Romana Visigothorum*, also known as the *Breviary of Alaric*, was issued in 506 by King Alaric.[32] It is cited as LRV or *Brev*. All these compilations drew on much the same materials, the Theodosian Code, the Codes of Gregorius and Hermogenianus, Gaius' *Institutes*, original or epitomized, the *Opinions* of Paul, and a few other post-classical versions of the jurists.

Pre-Justinianic jurisprudence

Gaius

The *Institutes* (or *Institutions*) of Gaius is easily the most important of the surviving juristic writings from the pre-Justinianic era, because of two things: it is the only almost-complete work from the classical period of law which has come down to us free from the editing of Justinian's compilers; and, through Justinian's *Institutes*, it has profoundly influenced the development of legal systems in Europe and further afield. The *Institutes* is an elementary intro-duction to Roman law, the law of the time – AD 160 or so – a time of high juristic activity. It is relatively systematic. After a few intro-ductory sentences on the sources of law (in the sense of our chapter 1), the rest of Book 1 deals with the law of persons, covering status, the manumission of slaves, paternal power, and tutory. Books 2 and 3 deal with *res*, things in which a person could have a proprietary interest; these are divided into heritable and moveable property (including servitudes), testate succession, intestate succession, and obligations (contract and delict). Book 4, with an excursus on the older form of procedure by actions in the law, deals with procedure under the formulary system, including interdicts; even this must have been largely obsolete. Gaius is the chief source for Justinian's *Institutes*, both in content and, more importantly, in system.[33] Because it talks of what were, for Justinian, long obsolete institutions and procedure, we can have a better idea of what changes from the classical law were made by the compilers.

Until the discovery at Verona in 1816 of a palimpsest – a re-used manuscript where the original writing (in this case Gaius) has been over-written – dating from the fifth century, Gaius was only known through an epitome attached to the *Lex Romana Visigothorum* and intended to represent extant law.[34] The Verona palimpsest made a critical edition possible; unfortunately early chemical attempts to bring up the over-written text have destroyed some of what could once be read. Subsequent editions are based on Studemund's exact copy, known as the *Apographum*,[35] culminating in the seventh edition of P. Krüger and W. Studemund in 1923, with a full critical apparatus.[36] Seckel and Kübler's Teubner seventh edition of 1935 used the discoveries of fragments in 1927 and 1933;[37] the most recent edition has been produced at Leiden by M.David & H.L.W.Nelson (1954–68); a commentary is in progress from Nelson and U.Manthe. Gaius' *Institutes* are normally cited simply as G. or Gaius, and by book and sentence. The most recent translation into English is that of Gordon and Robinson.[38]

Pauli Sententiae[39]

The *Opinions* of Paul were described by Schulz[40] as a pocket-*Digesta*, an encyclopaedic handbook used by practitioners. It dealt with many aspects of the law, including a fair number of titles on criminal matters. It is now generally held to have been put together, from various authentic writings of Paul, at the end of the third century or the very beginning of the fourth, a period when Diocletian was still maintaining the overall standards of classical law; it was approved by Constantine.[41] No independent manuscript of it survives; it must be reconstructed from the Germanic codes (particularly the *Lex Romana Visigothorum*), other post-classical works (such as the *Collatio*, FV, and the *Consultatio*), or the Digest. Cujas produced a critical edition in 1586; the text along with its Visigothic *interpretatio* is printed in Haenel's *Lex Romana Wisigothorum*, but the usual modern editions by Krüger and by Seckel and Kübler lack the *interpretatio*.[42] A parchment folio, the Leiden fragment, was discovered relatively recently, and it at least seems to come from an early period, close to Paul.[43] Because versions of a text quite often survive both within and outside the Digest, they can be a control on the changes made there. It is cited as PS, by book, title, and sentence. There is no reliable translation into English.

Epitome *of Ulpian*[44]

The work known commonly as the *Epitome* of Ulpian, or *Epitome of the Regulae* of Ulpian, is an elementary treatise dealing with persons, property and succession. It has come to us through a tenth-century manuscript which Cujas saw and Savigny rediscovered in the Vatican Library; this was an appendix to the *Lex Romana Visigothorum*.[45] Krüger produced an edition in 1878, but the modern edition is that of Schulz.[46] It was held by Schulz to be an epitome made soon after 320 not of Ulpian, but of an early post-classical writer, who had relied heavily on Gaius. He thought it faithful to its original as far as it went, but to have omitted much. Other opinion holds that it is probably indeed an epitome of Ulpian's *Regulae*;[47] others that it was a compilation of the fourth century.[48] The editors of FIRA preferred to entitle it *Tituli ex corpore Ulpiani*, a title rejected by Schulz. It is cited sometimes as EU, sometimes just as Ulpian (in the way just 'Gaius' means his Institutes), sometimes as *Ulp. Reg.* and by title and sentence. It was translated by Muirhead together with Gaius.[49]

Fragmenta Vaticana[50]

The Vatican Fragments is so-called because it is another palimpsest from the fourth or fifth century which was discovered in the Vatican in 1821. Mommsen produced a critical edition in 1860.[51] There seems to be only about a seventh (or perhaps much less) of the original; it was probably written shortly after 318.[52] It is an encyclopaedia of juristic writings and imperial legislation for the use of practising lawyers; inscriptions give the sources from which the extracts were taken. The surviving contents deal at some length with sale, usufruct, dowry, excuses from tutory, gift, and legal representatives. Again, it seems most likely that it largely reflects classical law, or the immediate post-classical period, for it refers to

such things as the tutory of women and conveyance by mancipation. It is cited as Fr.Vat. or FV, by sentence; there is no reliable
translation.

Mosaicarum et Romanarum Legum Collatio[53]

The *Collatio* (or Comparison) is part of a compilation, apparently
from the jurists mentioned in the Law of Citations together with
some imperial enactments, each title hung on a text from the
Septuagint. There is no agreement about why it was linked with
Mosaic law, and by whom. What survives of what was clearly a much
longer work are sixteen titles, fourteen on criminal law, with one
on deposit (based on the question of the depositee's liability for
theft) and another on intestate succession (where there appears to
be no criminal interest). It was first edited in the sixteenth century,
but two more manuscripts were discovered in the nineteenth
century; the oldest manuscript dates from the ninth century.
Bluhme produced an edition in 1833, but the standard modern
edition is Mommsen's, appearing in the *Collectio*.[54] The *Collatio*,
which is also titled *Lex Dei quam praecepit Dominus ad Moysen* in
some of the manuscripts, is cited as *Collatio* (or as *Coll.*) by title
and sentence. A translation by M.Hyamson was published by the
Oxford University Press in 1913. The greater part seems to reflect
the existing state of affairs at the beginning of the fourth century,
but the inclusion of an enactment of 390 has led to argument as
to whether this was an isolated addition.

Other juristic works

Other fragments have survived of juristic works. Some are
specifically attributed to a classical jurist, such as the extracts
allegedly from Papinian's *responsa* and *quaestiones*,[55] the *regulae* of
Modestinus,[56] and the *Sententiae et epistulae Hadriani*;[57] comparable
is the *Apokrimata*, or Decisions of Septimius Severus on Legal
Matters.[58] A useful work called *De Notis*, ascribed to Valerius Probus,
a grammarian of the late first century AD, gives various standard
abbreviations.[59] Other works are explicitly from a later period, such
as the *Consultatio veteris cuiusdam iurisconsulti*, normally cited
as *Consultatio*. It was first edited by Cujas; the modern edition
is Krüger's in the *Collectio*.[60] It is primarily concerned with the force
of various pacts, mostly in the field of family law; it probably dates

from the fifth century, but the manuscript seen by Cujas has been lost. Then there is the *Fragmentum Dositheanum*, a collection of passages for translation from Greek into Latin which includes a section on manumission, the grant of liberty to a slave. The only full edition, including the Greek text, is that of Böcking.[61] Various other manuscript fragments deal with such things as fiscal law, and cognatic relationships.[62]

Then, from the East, there are the *Scholia Sinaitica*, so-called because the manuscript is from a Sinai monastery;[63] the fragments are part of a commentary in Greek on Ulpian *ad Sabinum*, probably of the late fifth century. The *Syro-Roman Lawbook*[64] is the other work which has survived despite Justinian's prohibition on the use of anything prior to his codification; it seems to have been used in the law school of Beirut.

THE LITERARY SOURCES

As we have already remarked, much of our knowledge of what are strictly 'legal' sources comes through sources that are not themselves legal, but literary or technical. Nearly all of these rely upon a conventional manuscript tradition, a source valued when it was written, preserved through recognition of its value, and having similar problems concerning the editing of the manuscript. For example, we learn far more of the *leges regiae* from historians than jurists. We have extracts from Dionysius of Halicarnassus, Plutarch, Livy, even Tacitus, all historians of Rome, and from Festus, Macrobius, the elder Pliny, Servius (on Vergil), Lydus (*de mensibus*), grammarians, antiquarians, and encyclopaedists, not to mention Cicero (*de re publica*); there is one Digest excerpt.[65]

The Twelve Tables, so important psychologically to the Romans, again come to us through a variety of literary sources, as well as Gaius, who wrote a commentary on them, and other juristic citations.[66] Much of their content is known from quotations from them by Cicero, Gellius, and Festus. Other sources are Varro, Livy, Dionysius of Halicarnassus, the elder Pliny, Seneca, Tacitus, Quintilian, Apuleius, Macrobius, Nonius, Sidonius Apollinaris, Salvian, St Augustine, Isidore, and others – even the poet Horace. Gothofredus attempted a restoration in 1653; the basic modern edition remains that of Dirksen, revised by Schöll for the Teubner edition, which is closely followed by Bruns, Girard, and FIRA.[67] There are reasonable English translations.[68]

Other specifically legal texts have also been preserved in literary sources. Of statutes, for example, Festus is our source for the *lex Silia de ponderibus*, the *lex Papiria de sacramentis*, and the *lex Sulpicia rivalicia*, Censorinus for the *lex Plaetoria* on jurisdiction, and Gellius for the *lex Atinia de usucapione*.[69] The *lex Julia agraria* (of 59 BC?) is from a technical work on land surveying.[70] Frontinus, as water commissioner, tells us of the *lex Quinctia* on aqueducts,[71] and also of certain resolutions of the Senate on the water supply.[72] Other such resolutions are preserved in the literary sources, for instance, Suetonius' preservation of the words of the SC expelling philosophers and rhetoricians in 161 BC or the censors' edict against them in 92 BC.[73] Other examples, where we have what purport to be the actual words, are Cicero on the senatorial bills of ?51 BC,[74] or Macrobius on the renaming of the month of *Sextilis* as August.[75] All the remaining legislative acts collected in FIRA i are either from papyri (only thirteen of them, including the *Forma Idiologi*) or inscriptions, and the great majority are inscriptions.

Then there are other works about the role of law, although not written by lawyers, or about law and administration. Notable among these, although more concerned with the ideal than the actual, is the *de legibus* of Cicero, and also his *de re publica*. (Of a very different kind is the fascinating insider account of the sixth-century civil service in John Lydus' *de magistratibus*.) Very important in their (inevitably biased) way are Cicero's forensic speeches; there are also legal issues in some of his philosophical writings, and in many of his letters.[76] All these are illuminating, providing we take note of their context. Pliny the Younger too was a busy practising orator in the Roman courts, and as a source of information he must have the benefit of the doubt. His letters, although written for publication, deal with situations where his audience would share too much of his knowledge, both background and of particular cases, for more than a slight slant to be imposed. His tenth book, the exchange of letters when he was governor of Bithynia with the Emperor Trajan, are a first-hand source for provincial government.[77] Occasionally relevant are the works of rhetoricians like Quintilian, but they must be used with much caution, because it is clear that their forensic problems are grounded in traditional Greek-based rhetoric.

Other literary works also have a legal content. The historians of the Republic, that is, particularly Livy and Dionysius of Halicarnassus, naturally refer to legal matters in the context of political history; Livy gives information on legislation and, with more enthusiasm, on trials. The historians, however, are not reliable when dealing with the period before approximately 200 BC. They were not only using annalists with family scores to make, but also providing propaganda for the new regime;[78] some of their 'history' is probably pure invention, some is undoubtedly a back-projection of events of the later second and earlier first centuries. The Twelve Tables must, in some form, be accepted, but the onus of proof for the early Republic should be on whoever wants to claim anything as true. From around 200 BC we come to contemporary writings, such as Cato on agriculture and Plautus' comedies (much less useful is Terence, who didn't make many legal jokes). Cato tells us about farming contracts, and Plautus, although his outline plots are purely Greek, puts in straight Roman jokes, quite a few of them referring to petty courts.[79] Then there are the grammarians, antiquarians, encyclopaedists, men such as Varro and Festus, Pliny the Elder and Aulus Gellius, who give us much incidental information on legal matters – as we have seen with the Twelve Tables.[80]

The historians of the Empire, particularly Tacitus, give us much information about law, both legislation and trials; they were especially interested in criminal law, but unfortunately not in the details of its procedure. For example, Tacitus does not make clear whether Appuleia Varilla was tried before the *quaestio de adulteriis*, and he is also unhelpfully vague about the survival of the *quaestio de falsis* into the later first century.[81] Their utility is different from that of the Republican historians; their facts may be true but the interpretation put on them is clearly not to be taken at face value. The hidden agenda of Suetonius and Tacitus, and of Dio Cassius, must always be remembered. The author of the SHA weaved many fantasies, but some facts mentioned are true – we are here in an area almost as murky as the early Republic. Ammianus actually has a digression discussing lawyers – unfavourably.[82] Even the poets can give us information.[83] In chapter 5 we shall discuss the two interesting cases where we have both a legislative inscription and a historian's view, that is, the Bacchanalian conspiracy of 186 BC,[84] and Claudius' speech in the Senate, opening its membership to suitable Gauls.[85]

OTHER SOURCES: INSCRIPTIONS, PAPYRI, ETC.[86]

A vast number of inscriptions have survived[87] – not surprisingly, in
that stone and bronze are durable materials, but even so most of
them are damaged. Inscriptions of all sorts are recorded in the
massive *Corpus Inscriptionum Latinarum* and *Corpus Inscriptionum
Graecarum*, which aim to be complete collections. There are also
the still very useful selections of Dessau and Dittenberger. A
useful, if dated, work of reference is de Ruggiero's *Dizionario
Epigrafico*. Current finds are recorded or published in the journals
L'Année Epigraphique, IURA, and *Studia et Documenta Historiae Iuris*.
Much legislation, *leges* of the assemblies,[88] resolutions of the
Senate, imperial edicts, was published in this form because of its
permanence. Of the 108 legislative documents in FIRA i (that is,
excluding the *Leges regiae* and the Twelve Tables) thirteen are from
manuscripts and thirteen from papyri; all the rest are inscriptions.
We have mentioned the SC *de Bacchanalibus* of 186 BC and the
lex Irnitana as particularly interesting examples of legislation
recorded in this way.

There are many regulatory inscriptions. Some are simple, for
example the boundary stones defining public areas such as the
Campus Martius (put up by Augustus) or the banks of the Tiber
(put up in 8 BC by the consuls on the authority of the Senate).[89]
Others are more elaborate, such as the dedication of a sacred
grove around 240 BC:

> In this grove no person shall tip out dung nor cast down a
> dead body nor honour his deceased ancestors. If anyone acts
> contrary to this, against him let whosoever wishes raise an
> action in the law by the laying on of a hand – just as against
> someone judicially condemned – for the sum of 50 coins. Or
> it is permitted for a magistrate to fine him if he wishes.[90]

Apart from legislation, there are enormous numbers of inscriptions, funerary or honorific, recording families and careers. These
reveal the chances of political or military life; they also provide
some sort of statistical base for domestic history, and the facts of
marriage, birth, and death. However, funerary inscriptions in
particular have some tendency to come from rather narrow strata
in society, the upper classes, and the slaves and freedmen of the
upper classes. The strictly legal information they can give must
be trawled for, but is informative, especially cumulatively. For

instance, we can get confirmation about the restrictions on clubs and guilds, and also see something of the functioning of the shows and spectacles at Rome, from a common sepulchre of a guild of musicians in the first century which had the following inscription:

> To the shades of the gods.
> For the college of the band-players who are available for sacred and public [performances], whom the Senate has permitted to assemble, meet and come together for the sake of the games, in accordance with the Julian Act on the authority of Augustus.[91]

Quite common was the prohibition on the sale of a tomb or its inclusion with an estate going to an heir outside the family. Such a prohibition on the alienation of a tomb or other monument might lay down a fine – to be paid to the Vestal Virgins or the treasury, or to the city of Aquileia, where the informer was to receive a quarter of the fine.[92] These inscriptions illuminate the distinction between family (people who share one's blood) and external heirs which is a regular feature of the law of succession, especially of trusts – *fideicommissa*. Some inscriptions on tombs reflect pious hopes: 'let nobody urinate here', even if others had rather more chance of observance: 'It is not permitted to apply fire to this monument'.[93]

Inscriptions were normally less suitable for daily legal business, but they can be found dealing with wills, mancipations, gifts, and contracts.[94] They could also report judicial decisions. Bringing together problems of religious land and of ownership is the well-known record (in marble) of a judgment given – the *sententia Senecionis* – by the Sub-Prefect of the Misenum fleet where the father of one Aelius Rufinus had bought land and buildings from the heirs of a certain Patulcus Diocles. There was no problem about the buildings, but unfortunately it turned out that there were burials scattered throughout the fields, and so they were not susceptible of sale; however, since Rufinus, father and son, although without lawful title, had been in quiet possession of the fields, Senecio refused the Patulci's claim to their ownership.[95]

Even more numerous are the papyri, and very many of them record legal transactions, although there is argument as to how far they reflect Roman law or provincial practice. They are predominantly in Greek, and from the eastern Empire; particularly rich sources have been discovered in Egypt. Nevertheless, the opinion of recent scholars is that they are a suitable guide, if used

with caution, to Roman law.[96] Important collections of legal papyri
were made in the earlier twentieth century by Mitteis and by
Meyer, and a selection, with translation as well as text, by Hunt and
Edgar. Journals which try to keep abreast of papyrological finds
with a legal interest include *Journal of Egyptian Archaeology, Journal
of Juristic Papyrolgy, Revue Historique de Droit français et étranger*, and
also *IURA* and *SDHI*.

Papyri often include procedural matters; things which were of
their nature passing, even if a record was wanted for a decade or
two. Because of the very nature of the material, there is relatively
little directly on public law preserved in the papyri, although they
do include local directions issued by governors or their deputies,
and other administrative details. Thus, in addition to the paper-
work concerning litigation, the papyri contain mainly private
instruments.[97] For example, the will of a veteran from the fleet,
made in AD 191, starts with the simultaneous manumission and
institution of two female slaves as his heirs, mentioning that they
were both over 30 (which was to satisfy the Aelian Sentian Act and
permit them to become citizens at once), substitute heirs were
named, the daughter of one of the heirs (presumably his own
daughter) was to be free and receive a legacy, and suitable arrange-
ments were to be made for his funeral; there is a note that the will
was opened and read three years later, at the tax office for the
collection of the 5 per cent taxes on inheritances and on manu-
missions.[98] In contrast to such correct legality, another Egyptian
record, of AD 166, shows the sale of a boy slave, but, although both
parties to the sale seem to have been citizens, his conveyance was
by simple delivery, which would not give full *ius civile* ownership;
the promise for compensation for eviction in this case was for the
simple price.[99] Other obligations, such as a contract for transport
of vegetables along the Nile, reveal the law as described to us by the
jurists being put into action.[100]

Egypt was the source of most papyrus, so it is hardly surprising
that it was so much used there. But even in Egypt,[101] and far
more in the rest of the Empire,[102] the records of actual dealings
between ordinary persons were habitually written on wax covered
tablets with a stylus; it is surprising how many have survived. Their
format was commonly a diptych, and often only one half remains.
Significant groups of such documents have been found at Pompeii
and Herculaneum,[103] and also in places like Transylvania,[104] or
Vindolanda on Hadrian's Wall.[105]

For example, we have the copy (on a wax tablet) of an entry in the register of births of AD 62, mentioning the Papian Poppaean and Aelian Sentian Acts which governed respectively marriage and the achievement of citizenship for informally manumitted slaves (Junian Latins):

> 23 July, AD 62, at Alexandria in Egypt. Copied and checked from the register of declarations of the births of children, a register placed in the Atrium Magnum, in which was written that which follows:
> L. Julius Vestinus, Prefect of Egypt, has entered the names of those who, in accordance with the Papian Poppaean Act and the Aelian Sentian Act, have registered children born to themselves: L. Valerius (son of Lucius) Pollia Crispus ?375,000 HS?, a son born to him and Domitia (daughter of Lucius) Paulla, on 29 June AD 61, [and called] L. Valerius (son of Lucius) Pollia Crispus, now a Roman citizen from the 1st July.[106]

A will made in Egypt in AD 142 shows a cavalryman called Antonius Silvanus following the correct forms, beginning with the institution of the heir, and the disherison of any others who would have been heirs on intestacy, the requirement for formal acceptance of the inheritance, the naming of substitute heirs, the making of legacies, and the manumission of a slave under a condition.[107] Among the Transylvanian finds are documents recording sales. This example contrasts with the papyrus cited above on the sale of the Egyptian boy, and evidences the formal sale and delivery of a slave-girl in AD 139:

> Maximus Batonis bought and accepted by mancipation from Dasius for 205 *denarii* a slave-girl named Passia, or whatever else she is called, of around six years. He warrants this girl to be healthy, free from liability for theft or other delict, and not a runaway or a wanderer; if anyone should evict Maximus Batonis, or anyone to whom the interest in her comes, from this girl or any share of her so that he does not own and possess her lawfully, then, to Maximus Batonis requiring his faithful promise, Dasius promised faithfully to give Maximus Batonis the price of the girl and as much again.
> For this girl, as is written above, I, Dasius, have received and have 205 *denarii* from Maximus Batonis.[108]

Occasionally legal transactions survive in conventional manu-scripts.[109] Other information on legal matters, and also warnings to passers-by, may come from graffiti.[110] The famous cartoon (in the modern sense) from Samnite Aesernia shows the performance of the contract for a night's lodging: the man says to the landlady of the inn: 'Let's settle up', and he is charged an *as* for bread and wine, 2 *asses* for meat, 8 for the services of a girl, all of which he agrees, but he is outraged at the demand for 2 *asses* for his mule's hay.[111] Coins[112] tend to be more illuminating for public than private law; they were often used as constitutional as well as political statements in both Republic and Empire. The proven washing of base coins with silver throws light on commercial trans-actions, as well as on the criminal law.[113] Archaeological evidence also is more inclined to illuminate public law[114] but use can be made of it. For example, at a trivial level, the existence of collars for errant slaves is proved from their actual survival, but archaeology is also informative about the layout of urban property, which can help our understanding of a significant area of contract.[115] Furthermore, the law of burials would be much poorer without the aid of archaeological evidence.[116]

While it seems unlikely that any major manuscript will ever surface, it is not impossible that further passages will be found, comparable to the fragments of Gaius which were discovered in the 1930s. Inscriptions are constantly being unearthed, and although most of them merely confirm our pattern of knowledge, there have been major discoveries such as the *tabula Irnitana*.[117] Papyri too and tablets are still being discovered, and many of those already found have not yet been edited. So the sources of Roman law continue to grow, even if mostly in a small way.

NOTES

1 A list of comitial legislation, with the sources from which it is derived, is conveniently found in Rotondi (1912).

2 FIRA i and iii documents, apart from the *Leges regiae* and the Twelve Tables, are normally referred to by document number rather than page reference; that is the usage in this book.

3 The third long-accepted handbook collection of sources is that of Bruns, but it is rather out of date.

4 In the preliminaries to the Digest, *c. Dedoken* s. 18 refers to Julian's reduction 'in parvo libello'; cf. Gellius 11.17; ILS 8987 also refers to the praetor's *volumen*.

5 Lenel (1927); he was also responsible for the *Palingenesia Iuris Civilis*

(1889), which rearranges the juristic texts so as to recreate as far as possible the original books.

6   A Visigothic epitome of these codes is given in FIRA ii pp. 653–79; Krüger attempted a reconstruction in *Collectio*, vol. III.

7   See ch. 1.

8   For an introduction, see ELH, ch. 3.

9   See ELH, ch. 10, for the background.

10   I: Institutes, ed P. Krüger; Digest, ed T.Mommsen, revised Krüger; II: Code, ed Krüger; III: Novels of Justinian, ed R.Schöll & W.Kroll. W.Kunkel produced a new edition in 1954, incorporating corrections made to the *editio maior* and to previous editions of the stereotype; he excised, however, most of the indications of interpolations made by Krüger in his later editions. There have been a number of reprints. The new German translation, with text, by Behrends et al., is taking account of the most recent views on textual criticism.

11   This is particularly true – unfortunately – of Scott (1932).

12   Schulz (1953), p. 305f., argues that the Paraphrase of Theophilus, ostensibly on Justinian's Institutes, was based on an existing Greek version of Gaius used at the law school of Constantinople.

13   Thomas (1975); an older version is that of Lee (1956). There is a more recent translation, without commentary, by Birks & MacLeod (1987).

14   It is to this edition of the Digest that the *VIR* refers; the stereotype is usable with the *VIR* because there are marginal references to every fifth line in the *editio maior*, as 250, 15 for vol. 1 and 250,[15] for vol. 2.

15   Ed. P. Bonfante and others; it is in a small format.

16   Except that books 30–32 are not divided into titles, and each has the rubric *de legatis et fideicommissis*.

17   University of Pennsylvania Press, 1985. This is printed as a facing page translation opposite the *editio maior*. Monro's translation of books 1–15 is also generally reliable.

18   Edited by Heimbach (Leipzig 1833–50, with prolegomena, 1870) and with supplements; there is a new edition of the text and its *scholia* by H.J.Scheltema with subsequent scholars, such as D.Holwerda and N. van der Wal (Groningen 1953–88).

19   Schulz (1953), p. 146f., gives the two lists.

20   Bluhme (1820).

21   See Honoré (1978), and, above all, Mantovani (1987) who produces a more elegant version of the division into 'masses'.

22   See ch. 1.

23   *Collectio*, III.

24   FIRA ii pp. 653–65; two of the appendices to the LRV also contain some material from them – FIRA ii pp. 667–79.

25   Published posthumously in 1665, and re-published with additional notes in 1736–45; it is still very useful.

26   These Novels, while published in the same volume, were actually edited by P.M.Meyer. On Mommsen and CTh, see Croke (1993).

27   CTh 1.1.6, AD 435.

28   CTh 1.1.5, AD 429.

29 For example, the text of PS 1.15, cited in ch. 2, comes to us through the LRB. See Jolowicz, 466–8; ELH 1.5.

30 Vismara (1967); it was also edited by Bluhme for MGH *Leges* I.5, and reproduced in FIRA ii pp. 681–710. See also Schott (1979).

31 Edited by L.R. de Salis for MGH *Leges* I.2, and reproduced in FIRA ii pp. 711–50.

32 Edited by G.F.Haenel (Leipzig 1849, repr. 1962); only the appendices are reproduced in FIRA ii pp. 667–79.

33 It is uncertain whether Gaius invented this system of persons, things, actions – the people using the law, what they are concerned with, and how they deal with them, or who, what, how. On its later importance, mediated through Justinian's Institutions, see the Introduction in Birks & MacLeod (1987).

34 FIRA ii pp. 231–57.

35 *Gai institutionum commentarii quattuor*, published in Leipzig 1873, 4th edn, Berlin 1899.

36 In *Collectio*; with it are printed the Autun fragments – FIRA ii pp. 207–28. These are from a (probably) fifth century commentary on Gaius, written presumably by a professor at Autun.

37 FIRA ii pp. 201–4 (A.S. Hunt, P. Oxy xvii.2103) on which see Levy (1928), and de Zulueta (1928); FIRA ii pp. 195–200, from Arangio-Ruiz (1934) & (1935), on which see de Zulueta (1934–6).

38 W.M.Gordon & O.F.Robinson, Duckworth, 1988; this uses the Teubner edition, and is simply a translation. De Zulueta's *The Institutes of Gaius* I, text with critical notes and translation (Oxford 1946), & II, commentary (Oxford 1953) is a proper edition and still excellent, but his translation is somewhat difficult for students who have no Latin.

39 FIRA ii pp. 317–417. Other fragments attributed to Paul are given in FIRA ii pp. 419–32.

40 Schulz (1953), p. 176; see also Levy (1945).

41 CTh 1.4.2, AD 327/8. Levy (1945) and (1951) held that there was much alteration of the text in the fourth and fifth centuries; cf. Buckland (1944), who maintained that the contents essentially reflect classical law.

42 *Collectio*, II; *Iurisprudentia*.

43 David & Nelson (1955); edited by Archi, David et al. as *Studia Gaiana* IV (1956); see also Serrao (1956).

44 FIRA ii pp. 261–301.

45 Other fragments of works ascribed to Ulpian are given in FIRA ii pp. 303–16.

46 Krüger in *Collectio*; Schulz (1926).

47 As in *Textes*. See also Buckland (1924).

48 But Nelson (1981), pp. 80–96, has demonstrated that the theory of an epitome is preferable to that of a new compilation using Gaius and others.

49 Muirhead (1880).

50 FIRA ii pp. 461–540.

51 A corrected edition appears in *Collectio*, III; it was adopted and amended by Kübler in *Iurisprudentia*, 6th ed, 1927.

52 Schulz (1953), p. 311; Raber (1965).

53 FIRA ii pp. 541–89.

54 *Collectio*, vol. III; it was also adapted by Kübler for *Iurisprudentia*, vol. II, 6th edn, 1927.

55 FIRA ii pp. 433–46.

56 FIRA ii pp. 447–50.

57 Böcking (1837–44), I 192–214; Schiller believed it genuine – (1978), p. 42, fn. 6, citing himself (1971).

58 Ed. Westermann & Schiller (1954).

59 FIRA ii pp. 451–60; e.g., SPQR for *Senatus populusque romanus*, or DCS for *de consilii sententia*.

60 *Collectio*, vol. III; also in *Iurisprudentia* II, 6th edn, 1927. See also FIRA ii pp. 591–613.

61 Böcking (1837–44) I 192–200 & 214–28. The Latin is also printed in *Collectio*, *Iurisprudentia*, and FIRA ii pp. 615–21. See also Honoré (1965).

62 FIRA ii pp. 623–34; critical editions are to be found in *Collectio* and *Iurisprudentia*.

63 FIRA ii pp. 635–52.

64 FIRA ii pp. 751–98, ed. Furlani; cf. Selb (1990).

65 D 11.8.2, Marcellus 28 *dig*.

66 From Ulpian, Paul, Papinian, Marcian, Pomponius, Tryphoninus, Callistratus, Modestinus, also PS, the *Epitome* of Ulpian, and Justinian's Institutes; imperial rescripts also cited them occasionally.

67 Dirksen (1824) and Schöll (1866). All the editions mentioned give the sources for the individual laws.

68 Warmington (1967), pp. 424ff., gives text and translation, ARS just a translation.

69 FIRA i 1, 2 & 5 = ARS no. 10, 11 & 57; FIRA i 4 = ARS no. 18.

70 FIRA i 12 = ARS no. 91; see Cary (1929). Cf. FIRA i 54 = ARS no. 127.

71 All these *leges*, including the XII T, and some others found in the literary sources, are newly edited in *Roman Statutes* vol. II.

72 FIRA i 14 & 41 = ARS no. 141 & 143; Frontinus *de aquis* 129; 100–1, 104, 106, 108, 125, 127.

73 FIRA i 32 & 52 = ARS no. 34 & 59; Suetonius *rhet.*1

74 Cicero *ad fam.* 8.8 includes FIRA i 37.

75 FIRA i 42 = ARS no. 145; Macrobius *sat.* 1.12.35.

76 On Cicero's contribution to our knowledge of law, see particularly Costa (1927), and Greenidge (1901).

77 See Williams (1990); Sherwin-White (1966); Hardy (1889).

78 A brief discussion of this kind of propaganda can be found in O.F.Robinson's review of P. Giunti, *Adulterio e leggi regie*, in *Gnomon* 64 (1992).

79 E.g. Plautus *Aulul.* 416ff.; *Curc.* 470–86; *Rudens* 373–4; *Stich.* 352. See Duckworth (1952), especially ch. 14; I cannot believe that the specific jokes in popular comedies would not reflect the world the audience knew.

80 Wenger (1953) 888–95 stresses the importance of literary information concerning religion in this context.

81 Tacitus *Annals* 2.50; 14.40–1.

82 Ammianus 30.4.1–22.

83 Horace, for example, is cited thirteen times in Robinson (1994), and four or five times in Robinson (1995).

84 FIRA i 30 = ARS no. 28 and Livy 39.8–19.

85 FIRA i 43 = ARS no. 175 and Tacitus *Annals* 11.25.

86 FIRA iii is devoted to this kind of legal source; we shall use it as our guide.

87 See Keppie (1991); see also the entry under Epigraphy in OCD.

88 These, including some *rogationes* – legislative proposals – are specifically the content of *Roman Statutes* vol. I.

89 FIRA iii 78 a); ILS 5923.

90 FIRA iii 71b) = ARS no. 14, 2.

91 FIRA iii 38.

92 E.g. FIRA iii 81a); iii 82k) and g).

93 FIRA iii 83h) and g).

94 Examples are FIRA iii 32–40, 42–5; 48, 53–6, 69–70; 71–86; 92–7; 106, 109–14, 116–18; 124 (cf. G 3.130); 145, 147, 152–3; 162–5, 185.

95 FIRA iii 86.

96 See most recently, Bagnall (1995); also Taubenschlag (1955).

97 Examples are FIRA iii 6–10, 12–24, 26–31; 46; 50–2, 57–8, 61–8; 98–105; 107–8, 115, 119; 121, 126; 132–3, 135–6, 138, 140, 142, 146, 148–9, 151, 154–6, 158–61; 166–84, 186–9.

98 FIRA iii 50. (No reference, however, was made to the provisions of the Fufian Caninian Act, which restricted the number of slaves who could be freed in a will – G 1.42–6.)

99 FIRA iii 132.

100 FIRA iii 155.

101 E.g. FIRA iii 1–5, 11, 25; 47, 59–60; 134.

102 E.g. FIRA iii 137 is from Frisia, and concerns the sale of a (presumably Friesian) bull or ox; iii 139 deals with the sale of a farm in Africa.

103 FIRA iii 91; 128–31. See Camodeca (1992); cf. Crook (1994b); see also Wolf & Crook (1989). For the Herculaneum tablets see generally Arangio-Ruiz (1974), for a collection of his papers and references to Pugliese Carratelli's editorial work. For the particular case of Justa, see Arangio-Ruiz (1948b & 1951 & 1959).

104 FIRA iii 87–90; 120, 122–3, 125; 150, 157. See Tomulescu (1971); Ciulei (1983).

105 On Vindolanda see Bowman & Thomas (1983) and (1986) and (1991); also Bahn (1992).

106 FIRA iii 2. There must be an error here in nomenclature, as the parents cannot both be citizens, entitled to filiation; while it is not impossible that one might have a father, the other a patron, both called Lucius, it seems more likely that the pair had been manumitted by the same Lucius, manumitted informally, which is why they needed to achieve citizenship by the birth of a child – Gaius 1.29–31.

107 FIRA iii 47.

108 FIRA iii 87; the signatures of the seven witnesses required for conveyance by mancipation were given on the fourth page of the triptych.

109 Examples are FIRA iii 49; 130–1 (chirographs); 141.

110 Examples are FIRA iii 127a; 143–4.

111 CIL IX 2689.
112 See Wenger (1953) 895–910; see also Crawford (1985); Mattingley (1960); cf. Nicolet (1994) at pp. 630–5.
113 Grierson (1956).
114 See Robinson (1994); see also, e.g. Bruun (1991); Lanciani (1888) or (1897); Tortorici (1991).
115 FIRA iii 127b; see Frier (1980); Wenger (1953) 878–88.
116 de Visscher (1963); Robinson (1975); Kaser (1978).
117 Gonzalez (1986); cf. Galsterer (1988) and Rodger (1991).

Chapter 4

The Settling of Disputes

INTRODUCTORY

Of course, no legal system is effective unless the law found in the sources can be put into practice. We have seen in our consideration of *negotia* that businessmen and even soldiers seem generally to have observed due legal forms in their daily transactions, that they knew the law well enough.[1] And educated Romans clearly knew more about legal procedure than do educated modern Europeans; Horace could write that the good man was not merely one who obeyed the law in all its forms, but who also acted as witness, stood surety, and performed as *iudex*.[2] This chapter is concerned with how citizens sought a remedy when there was a breakdown in these transactions, what procedures were available to them. The actual likelihood of success for the ordinary man will be considered in chapter 5.

The importance of the mechanics of Roman law is sometimes surprising to modern lawyers, most of whom are accustomed to codified legal systems. It ought not to be so surprising to the historian of the English Common Law where, to an even greater extent, the substance was shaped by the procedure. Nevertheless, few historians of the Common Law seem serious about Roman law; they often continue merely to see a misconceived analogy between the roles of the Urban Praetor at Rome and the Lord Chancellor in England, in spite of Buckland's demonstration of the Praetor's mastery of the whole range of civil procedure.[3]

Roman law went through three stages of procedure, of which the third, *cognitio*, was a reflection of the new political situation of the Empire, in which the power of cognoscing and of enforcement were held together; this stage did not play any particularly creative part in the development of law in ancient Rome. *Cognitio* was, however, the forerunner of nearly all modern European systems (and of those influenced by them, in Latin America, etc.) of civil procedure, although its actual transmission was largely through the canon law.

It was the two earlier stages, the *legis actiones* (actions in the law) and the formulary system, which had been themselves causative. Their limitations required that lawyers or jurists approach the problems of their clients in a way that would be successful – this is true of course for all lawyers – but what they had to say was 'my client's claim fits the action on sale, or the policy action on sale, or the action with a preliminary sentence (*actio prescriptis verbis*), in that he did this or his opponent did that'; neither for action in the law nor formula could one simply say, 'my client has a right'. For both of these stages we have a narrative account in Gaius; the whole of book 4 of his *Institutes* is devoted to procedure. Justinian's account of the law of actions is largely a paraphrase of information given in Gaius. He mentions a few reforms, passed by himself or his immediate predecessors,[4] but the persistence of the formulary model is evident; he even devotes a title to interdicts which ends with the remark that this is pointless – *supervacua* – since they are no longer used.[5] Therefore, lacking any single source for *cognitio*, we shall use at some length quotations from the *negotia* to illustrate its working.

THE *LEGIS ACTIONES*

In the time of the Twelve Tables and until some time after 200 BC the dominant form of civil procedure was by actions in the law. While the consuls were the original magistrates with jurisdiction, the office of praetor was specifically created to exercise this function in 367 BC; thereafter the praetor held the most important office in the state after the consuls. Someone who wished to make a claim, the pursuer (or plaintiff), conventionally known to Roman law as Aulus Agerius, summoned the defender, conventionally known as Numerius Negidius, simply by an oral request that he should come to court to appear before the Praetor. It was up to the pursuer to persuade or force a reluctant defender. It is assumed that this would normally work, even if the defender were more powerful, rich, or influential, because of the importance of a reputation as a good citizen in a shame culture, but sometimes clearly a defender will have simply ignored the pursuer.[6] If the (compliant) defender had good reason not to come at that time, he had to provide someone as a surety, called a *vindex*.

The parties appeared together, on those days on which court actions were permitted (*dies fasti*), before the Praetor, who was in charge of all civil jurisdiction.[7] This is the stage over which the magistrate exercised jurisdiction, called *in iure*; it was only the first stage of the procedure. The pursuer had to speak the appropriate form of his claim in set words, and the defender also replied in set words; this was the actual *legis actio*. The forms, as far as we know them,[8] are (all but one) abstract; but it is clear that a specific claim must have been included. While there is no evidence that a slip of the tongue was penalized, Gaius tells us that a man who wished to sue for the destruction of his vines lost his case because he used the word 'vines' rather than the 'trees' of XII T 8.11.[9]

Of the forms for pursuing a claim there were four:[10] (A) the action in the law by oath for a real right (*in rem*[11]), (B) the action in the law by oath for a personal right (*in personam*), (C) the action in the law by application for a judge (*iudex* or arbiter), and (D) the action in the law by action of debt. (A) could be used for land or a moveable, but the latter, or a token of the former, must be present in court, so that the parties could each lay a rod on it as a symbol of ownership; they then challenged each other with an oath, backed by a sum staked on the outcome. An undefended claim was *ipso facto* lost. The Praetor assigned interim possession to one party, demanding security from him; the Praetor had *imperium* and could enforce his orders. (B) seems to have been a simple assertion, again made with an oath, and backed by a sum staked – greater or less according to the value of the claim; here the defender must speak to admit or deny the claim, since there was nothing on the table for the pursuer to take. (C) was used in specific cases where statute had authorized it, as in an action on a stipulation (although it was not necessarily used here), or for partition actions where, since the parties were coming to court hand in hand to split an inheritance or other common property, there could be no place for an oath on the truth of the claim. Its great advantage was that the losing party did not risk forfeiting a substantial sum; 500 *asses* was the normal sum at stake in the action in the law by oath, although when someone's free status was at issue the sum staked was the same as for small claims, merely 50 *asses*. (D) was only introduced around 204 BC, by a Silian Act, for the recovery of a definite sum of money; it was extended by a Calpurnian Act to other definite things, for example, a slave, or 100 jars of the best Campanian wine, or the rent already due. The pursuer made his claim, and when the defender denied it, the pursuer summoned him for thirty days hence for the appointment of a *iudex*. The reasons for the introduction of (D) remain obscure. Why was it needed if, as is probable, the formula was beginning to come into use at this time? Moreover, it does not seem to have applied except where (B) or (C) could have been used. The conjecture seems plausible that (C) remained only available where statute specifically authorized it, and that (B) had become limited by juristic conservatism to legal transactions already recognized at the time of the Twelve Tables; thus it would not have covered either *mutuum* or the written contract. There was also a procedure *per sponsionem*, which was probably the result of juristic simplification. Instead of using (A), a claim to ownership could be subject to a small wager by stipulation, and it was the outcome of the wager which was in theory tried, not the question of ownership.

After the parties had exchanged their ritual, the question at issue was set; this was called joinder of issue (*litis contestatio*). Thereafter no fresh action could be brought by the same pursuer on the same facts; also, any heirs would inherit not only the claim but also the liability. The last act before the Praetor was the appointment, for the trial stage of the procedure, of a *iudex* or arbiter – probably the former where the question was simply whether or not there was liability, the latter when its extent must be determined. The origins of this divided procedure are un-known.[12] The Praetor was not a judge in the modern sense, nor (normally) a man specializing in the law, but he could expect, as a senior magistrate, to have the assistance of jurists to advise him, whether on his *consilium* or less formally. It was during the stage *in iure* that points of law were argued, whether there really was a legal claim, or whether on equitable grounds there should be.

The *iudex* – or *recuperatores* (arbiters) – to whom the case was sent thereafter was there to try the facts. A *iudex* was not a judge in the modern, or even later Roman, sense, but really a one-man jury, normally chosen from a list, itself selected from the upper classes. It is argued that the album from which the civil *iudex* was drawn was the same as for criminal juries, and therefore before the Gracchan reforms it was composed solely of senators; this seems to put a heavy burden on already busy men. There is no doubt that

Gracchus extended to equestrians membership of criminal juries, and that this membership shifted to and fro in the political battles of the late Republic. However, it is not clear that the list from which the Praetor chose civil *iudices* was equally affected. While recorded criminal trials were largely political, and therefore affected the senatorial class above all, civil actions will often have been between not only equestrians but also plebeians; expediency may therefore have left the enlarged album available. On the other hand, the right of choice of a *iudex* by the parties that we find in the classical law may have been available in the *legis actio* system; perhaps this was, indeed, normal practice,[13] for certainly the parties had both to agree to accept the *iudex*.

Two other sorts of court for the trial of facts seem to have been set up in connection with the actions in the law, the centumviral and the decemviral courts. Both go back at least the mid-third century BC. In the Republic the *decemviri slitibus iudicandis*, who were minor magistrates (members of the vigintisexvirate), sat individually; their competence was particularly over questions of free status. The centumviral court consisted in the later Republic of a panel of 105 qualified persons, from whom a jury was selected for each case; in the Republic ex-quaestors presided over these jury courts. In the Empire there were 180 on the panel, and there were normally four juries formed, presided over by the *decemviri*.[14] The centumviral court continued into the second century AD, as Pliny witnesses, to hear certain cases – claims to an inheritance (*hereditatis petitio*) and complaints that a will should be set aside as lacking in familial piety (*querela inofficiosi testamenti*) – begun by *legis actio*. It was the forum for the famous *causa Curiana*, when the noted jurist Q.Mucius Scaevola argued for a strict interpretation,[15] and the noted orator L.Licinnius Crassus for an equitable interpretation in a dispute over a will. It continued to feature cases attracting wide interest in Pliny's time; he tells us that it was the most exciting court for a forensic orator.

Anyway, the second stage was, properly speaking, a trial, an investigation into the facts. The *iudex* was free from restrictions about *dies nefasti* etc., and he could adjourn the case as necessary, and hear a case where he chose – although not in a tavern (at least in later law). He was not required to have a *consilium*, although one may have been usual; he could consult anyone he chose. Aulus Gellius tells us that on an occasion when he was *iudex* he consulted a philosopher as well as those learned in the law.[16]

Advocates often spoke for their clients; evidence was produced by both parties. Unless the *iudex* could swear that he was unable to reach a conclusion, he must give his judgment in the presence of both parties. If it was in favour of the pursuer, it may – as in the formulary system – have always been in a definite sum of money, although an arbiter (or board of arbiters) presumably estimated the sums awarded. (It is worth remarking that coined money appeared fairly late at Rome, probably first being minted there in the early third century BC, and so early judgments were presumably for a specific weight of bronze.) There was no appeal, as was also true in the formulary system; *intercessio* was technically possible against the Praetor in the earlier stage, but the *iudex* had been accepted by both parties through the *litis contestatio.*

Assume that the pursuer has won his case, in that the *iudex* has given judgment for him. How did he benefit? In partition actions it may have been the same as in the formulary system where the Praetor's *imperium* authorized the decision of the *iudex* to such an extent that quiritary ownership was settled by the division made. Presumably in actions *in rem* he could just walk away with his property, if he had had interim possession; in other cases, whether real or personal, he may have needed the action of the law by the laying on of a hand, to justify his arrest of his debtor. (The taking of a pledge as an action in the law was restricted to particular cases, such as the liability, strictly speaking owed to the state, of a widow to provide for a soldier's needs.) Execution was always against the person of the unsuccessful defender, the debtor as he had been proved, who became the bondsman of his creditor. Execution needed the authorization of a magistrate, but must be put into effect by the pursuer. Here again a pursuer who was socially or economically inferior to the defender must have had difficulties.

THE FORMULARY SYSTEM

The system of pleading by formulas, the formulary system, seems to have begun early in the second century BC. It is quite clear that it was the creation of the Praetor.[17] It largely replaced the actions in the law after an Aebutian Act which was passed some time between 145 and 120 BC; this process was completed by Augustus' *leges Iuliae iudiciorum,*[18] except insofar as the centumviral court continued to use certain actions in the law. The formulary system was therefore dominant from roughly 150 BC to say AD 150 or perhaps the end of the second century. *Cognitio* had, however, begun to replace it from the beginning of the Empire, although the formal abolition of the formulary system did not come until AD 342. In the formulary system the claims in abstract form were replaced by more specifically phrased forms of words (*concepta verba*), and this formula, which had been precised with great care in the stage *in iure*, was sent to the *iudex* who must, if the allegations in the formula were proven true, find the defender liable, but if he did not find them proven he must assoil (absolve) the defender.

It was still the pursuer's problem to get the defender to court; the defender could now promise by stipulation to appear before the Praetor on a certain day, without needing to provide a definite surety. The pursuer must make clear what his claim was, and when the parties appeared together before the magistrate he produced a draft formula, and requested the Praetor to grant him an action based on it. The defender might accept the formula proposed, or there might be argument on points of law leading to the formula's modification. The Praetor could exercise his *imperium* to make the parties agree, by denying the action to a pursuer who would not, for example, accept a defence (*exceptio*), or by ordering a defender to accept, under threat of arrest, a replication countering a defence. An *exceptio* was essentially a 'yes, but . . . ' form of defence; it was not a total denial, but a further fact or set of facts which invalidated the force of the basic claim (*intentio*).[19] Thus a pursuer might come to court claiming that the defender had not returned the plough ox he had borrowed; the defender might say by way of defence that it had been later agreed that he could keep the ox until the end of the next month, while the pursuer could put in a replication that they had subsequently agreed that the loan should only be for a week.[20] The use of *exceptiones* must have become much less frequent with the great growth of *bonae fidei iudicia*, actions where good faith was explicitly taken into account, such as that on the contract of sale. When the formula expressed what the parties agreed was the matter in dispute, then the Praetor appointed the *iudex*, and *litis contestatio* took place. The Praetor then issued his decree empowering the trial.

The Praetor in the earlier system of actions in the law may not have been able to refuse an action claimed in proper form, although it is possible that he could,[21] but he certainly came to be able to do so under the formulary system. Indeed, he made clear in his Edict that there were circumstances where he would not grant an action, between freedman and patron for example. On the other hand, a freedman might, say, have been sexually assaulted by his patron and wish to raise an action for outrage (*iniuria*), and in these circumstances, for particular reason shown (*causa cognita*), the normal refusal might be waived. Equally, the Praetor could state in the Edict that there was a formula for a situation not envisaged in the traditional *ius civile*. He might, for instance, offer a defence or a remedy – as appropriate – where there had been on the face of the matter an actionable *ius civile* claim but this had been brought about by fraud. A very famous example is the Publician action,[22] where the Praetor said he would grant an action to a pursuer claiming ownership of a piece of property when that pursuer was not yet the quiritary owner but only in the course of usucaping it, that is, he was on the way to becoming quiritary owner. (For usucapion the pursuer had to have acquired something in good faith and with grounds for good title, and then after possessing it unchallenged for a period of time – in classical law two years for land, one year for moveables – he would become the quiritary owner.) This action, with the fiction[23] that the period of usucapion had been completed, in effect undermined the traditional requirement for the cumbrous formal conveyance of certain sorts of property (*res mancipi*) which had been necessary for full ownership, and gave the advantages of being owner to someone who had acquired such property informally. This was within a range of remedies described as the Praetor aiding, supplementing, and correcting the *ius civile*.

Outside the Edict there were other methods to this end, such as praetorian stipulations and cautions. Wherever good faith seemed to demand it, the Praetor could require the giving of security by an enforceable stipulation. For example, the Praetor could refuse to allow a usufructuary into possession if she had not given security to the bare owner that his property would be returned to him in the same state as she had received it; this was the *cautio usufructuaria*. Similarly, with *damnum infectum*, the Praetor used his *imperium* to empower the potential victim of, say, a manure heap that might undermine his wall, to take possession of the threatening area of his neighbour's garden if the neighbour refused to do anything. Also based on good faith was the Praetor's power to restore matters to their original status (*restitutio in integrum*). For example, if someone was terrorized into formally conveying his farm to a villain, the Praetor could after investigation set aside the mancipation, or he could undo the legal effects of a contract into which a minor had been induced by fraud.

The Edict came to contain a wide range of formulas, based both on the *ius civile* and on praetorian development of the law; the *ius honorarium* could be described as the living voice of the *ius civile*.[24] It seems likely that granting an action was in most cases automatic where the parties agreed that they would go to trial on the basis of one of the formulas in the Edict. Indeed, only if actions were granted automatically could the two Praetors, Urban and Peregrine, have managed to cope with all the civil actions raised in Rome and its environs. The jurisdiction, for example, of the aediles over the markets did mean that there were some cases which did not need to be taken before the Praetor, but his juris- diction was not thereby excluded. In time the actions granted *edictal vs. decretal actions* automatically came to be known as edictal actions, while the cases which needed arguing before the Praetor would grant an action became known as decretal actions. For example, the edictal clause on the Aquilian Act promised a remedy for damage to property by burning or breaking – in terms of the statute; one day a pursuer must have come and asked for an action based on the Act because his neighbour had locked up a straying cow and allowed it to starve to death. Causing such a financial loss by an act of omission was not mentioned in the Act, or the Edict, so the pursuer, advised probably by a jurist, must have argued before the Praetor, who will also have been advised by a jurist, that it was an analogous situation; the Praetor therefore decreed an action. Decretal actions themselves clearly came to be granted automatically.

Another field where the Praetor's control of actions had a great impact on the usability of legal remedies was in the so-called adjec- titious actions. These made the transactions of slaves and of sons in paternal power enforceable against owner or father, the only member of the *familia*[25] with proprietary capacity; a slave naturally could not own anything, and children in paternal power could not either. It is worth stressing that a woman who was no longer in paternal power (and not in marital subordination – *manus* – which was already fading away in the Late Republic) had proprietary capacity; she could own slaves and would, as owner, be liable for their transactions. Paternal power was, however, strictly that; a mother had no ordinary legal authority over her children.

Areas of innovation – causa in factum concepta
– bona fides / metus
– vicarious liability
– equity (e.g. causa Publiciana); restitutio in integrum;
cautio damni infecti

When *litis contestatio* had been achieved and an action granted, the *in iure* stage of procedure was finished. The case, with its formula, went to the *iudex*, the one-man jury, or to arbitrators (*recuperatores*). The *iudex* had the formula to guide him. If it said that the pursuer claimed 10,000 and that if his claim appeared well founded the *iudex* was to condemn the defender for 10,000, then that was the *iudex'* choice, to condemn for 10,000 or to assoil. But it might say that the *iudex* was to condemn for the value of something, or whatever the matter seemed worth, or the amount that was due; it might limit him to a certain maximum (*taxatio*), or it might say that he was not to condemn for the value of property in dispute if, to his satisfaction, the defender restored it to the pursuer. Furthermore, partition actions continued, and in these the *iudex* was to assign property to the parties as seemed fair, and to even things up between them by ordering a money payment, where necessary. But the principle was that a condemnation was always in money terms.

Execution under the formula was somewhat different from the earlier system, although it was still an affair for the successful pursuer to put into effect. Except in real actions where the successful party was already in possession, the judgment creditor, before proceeding, had to raise an action on the judgment (*actio iudicati*) before the Praetor; if the defender wished to fight the judgment – perhaps because he challenged the jurisdiction, perhaps because he had already made satisfaction – then he must give security and became liable for double damages if he lost this round too. However, there was a change, in that execution was no longer always against the person, although this remained common throughout the Empire. Execution against the debtor's entire property became gradually more frequent. The Praetor would issue a decree putting the creditor in possession of the debtor's property as a whole (*missio in bona*); the pursuer must then announce this publicly so that other creditors could make their claims known. After thirty days the creditors elected one of their number to auction off the estate to the person who would pay the creditors the highest rate in the pound; this buyer could in turn pursue the judgment debtor's debtors. The process was roundabout, and inevitably made the debtor bankrupt. From the time of Augustus, a judgment debtor could voluntarily hand over his estate to be sold up; even though he was still made bankrupt, he did not incur infamy, nor was he liable to be made the creditor's bondsman.

examples

Three imaginary case histories

I: Let us say that Aulus Agerius has bought a slave, called Stichus, who turns out to be epileptic, from Numerius Negidius, who had just inherited him as part of his aged aunt Lucia's estate.

Aulus Agerius will argue that Numerius Negidius ought to pay damages for providing defective goods under the good faith contract of sale. Although the consensual contract of sale was introduced by the Praetor, it became classed as part of the *ius civile*. Numerius Negidius might argue that he had given no warranty as to the slave's health (this defence might not be sufficient under *cognitio* when such a warranty had become implicit); he might further point out that this had been a private, not a market, sale and so there was no strict liability under the edict of the curule aediles. Juristic interpretation allowed damages simply for the lesser value of the slave if the defect had been unknown – as seems probable here – while a dolose defender was liable to the pursuer for all consequential loss. The Praetor, the aediles, and the jurists are all sources for this drama, as well as what had been absorbed into the traditional law of Rome.

II: Let us say that Numerius Negidius has invented an automotive wheeled machine powered by sails; in the course of trying to test it he comes onto the property of Aulus Agerius. There he kills a horse, a pig, and a pet elephant, severely injures a slave, and knocks down a chicken shed, killing the occupants from shock.

Aulus Agerius will argue that Numerius Negidius has wrongfully caused him financial loss falling under the Aquilian Act. If Numerius Negidius argued that the Aquilian Act did not cover automotive machines, Aulus Agerius could ask for an action on the facts, such a machine being analogous to an out-of-control mule for which an unskilled mule driver would be responsible. Aulus Agerius would specify that he wished to claim the highest value in the past year of the three dead mammals, under chapter 1 of the Act; Numerius Negidius would admit that pigs as well as horses fell under that chapter, but argue that elephants did not. Aulus Agerius would claim under chapter 3 for his other losses, the actual diminution in the value of the slave and any medical expenses incurred, the cost of replacing the shed, and the value of the dead chickens; Numerius Negidius might argue that the death of the chickens from shock was too indirect to be his liability. In this drama we have a statute, and its interpretation – based on custom – to exclude elephants; we have the Praetor taking a positive role to allow for new but analogous circumstances, and there would be juristic argument on causation.

III: Let us say that Caelius Carinus, a young man in the paternal power of Numerius Negidius, has borrowed money from Aulus Agerius for buying books; let us say further that Numerius Negidius is himself in need of money because he promised a dowry to his niece, and he too has borrowed from Aulus Agerius, giving as surety his sister, Tertia Tullia.

Aulus Agerius claims that Caelius owes him money which Numerius Negidius should pay on account of the personal fund he has granted his son; he will be met by Numerius Negidius, on behalf of Caelius Carinus, for whose debts he would in many circumstances be liable, with the defence of the SC Macedonianum, that loans to sons in power are not recoverable; Aulus Agerius will counter with the argument that it had been accepted that loans for studying purposes were valid, but Numerius Negidius might reply that the books he saw were erotic not philosophical. Aulus Agerius might wish to sue Tertia Tullia, who is undoubtedly rich, rather than Numerius Negidius; he will be met with the defence of the SC Velleanum, making unenforceable personal security offered by a woman, which was seen as unbecoming to her sex. Aulus Agerius will then point to an imperial ruling that in the particular circumstances Tertia was acting in her own interests – her daughter's dowry – and so not covered by the SC Velleanum. Here we have custom, two resolutions of the Senate, an imperial ruling, and juristic interpretation of one of the resolutions.

COGNITIO

Just as *legis actiones* long co-existed with the formula, so the formula only gave way slowly to the third of the Roman systems of procedure, known as *cognitio*, although the word is really just another term for jurisdiction, the cognoscing of the judge as Scots law has it. The term therefore does not tell us anything about the procedure, but refers to the power of the magistrate or official. Although *cognitio* sprang from official power, indeed ultimately from the emperor's power, it was concerned with judicial process, and maintained much of the older approach. The chief difference with the new form of procedure was the active intervention of the state where previously the pursuer had had to take measures for himself, in summons and execution. Further, the official with *cognitio* was in charge of the whole process; he heard the pleadings and then the evidence as to the facts. Writing, rather than oral proceedings, steadily became required.

Cognitio was, indeed, the kind of jurisdiction normally exercised in the provinces of the late Republic;[26] it was an official's *cognitio extra ordinem*, outside the *ordo* – the *ordo* meaning the normal jurisdiction of the Praetor. Under Augustus there was a small but significant move at Rome itself from *iurisdictio* to *cognitio*, when the emperor told the consuls, not the Praetor, to enforce certain trusts (*fideicommissa*). In the course of the century *fideicommissa* generally became enforceable, but before the *cognitio* of a special appointed *praetor fideicommissarius*. Similarly, matters affecting tutories were passed over first to the consuls and then to a special praetor, not to the Urban Praetor. *Cognitio* was not one single form of procedure, but varied somewhat depending whether it sprang from the emperor and his immediate delegates, or from specific functions; also, not surprisingly, time brought about changes. For example, by the Later Empire litigation had become much more expensive, because, unlike the days of the Republic and Principate, advocates had to be paid, and there were court fees as well.

The summons – *denuntiatio* – was now issued by the pursuer to the defender with the backing of the court; if the defender lived in another jurisdiction, the pursuer obtained letters from the court addressed to the local magistrates who issued the summons.

> To Tiberius Claudius Areius, mayor of the district of Heraclis in the Arsinoite territory, Tabus, daughter of Teseis her mother, native of the Socnopaean Island village of the same district, having as tutor her son Stotoes, son of Apynch.
> There is a serious dispute between me and my full brother Satabus, which requires that justice which is applied within his whole jurisdiction by Pompeius Planta, the most noble Prefect. Satabus entered on this dispute with malice when, having brought into his counsels his confederate Harpogath, the son of another brother now dead, he appropriated for himself all the goods of Teseis, my deceased mother. Therefore I ask that a copy of this petition, entered in your records, be served by one of your officials on Satabus so that he may

know himself, together with Harpogath, to be summoned
wherever in this territory Pompeius Planta, the most noble
Prefect, shall hold an assize, and thus through you I shall be
succoured.
Subscription of the official: It was served by Ammonius, son
of Ammonius, the court officer. In the second year . . . [AD
99].[27]

And if the defender could not be found, the pursuer was authorized to put up a written notice of summons – rather like planning
permission applications. A Roman magistrate had always had
the right of summoning individual persons before him; now he
used this at the request of a private citizen. This power allowed for
judgment by default if the defender failed to answer after the usual
three (monthly) summons.[28]

In the eighth year [AD 89]. . . . Certain persons among those
on the published list of names cited to court did not reply,
and Mettius Rufus [the Prefect] ordered his herald to
proclaim: 'Let those who have been cited before me and not
replied know that they shall be summoned once more and
then, if they have still not replied, let them be condemned
in their absence.'
Apollodorus, the advocate: 'After your proclamation
Menelais, Posidonia and Posidonius, for whom I am acting,
give the necessary security that they cannot plead their cause
until they receive letters from their tutors, and they ask their
presence to be noted on the public record.' Mettius Rufus:
'It shall be noted.'[29]

If the pursuer failed to turn up on the day appointed, he inevitably
lost his case, unless reinstatement of time[30] was appropriate, as
where he had been absent on public service.

By Justinian's time the procedure had changed somewhat, and
there was a libel – a signed, written claim which the pursuer must
hand in to the court – to initiate an action; the pursuer must give
caution to bring the issue to *litis contestatio* within two months.[31]
The court then served the libel (if in correct form) on the defender,
who had to give security for his appearance, and who produced his
libellus contradictionis[32] – which of the pursuer's allegations were
accepted, and which were not known and not admitted. Great men
might start their actions by obtaining a rescript, which they then
took to the court for service on the defender.

The proceedings were no longer out of doors in the forum,[33] as had been the case in the older systems, but held within a court-room. The pleading stage seems to have continued much as with the formula, although there was more discretion in the court. To the statement of claim by the pursuer there were responses by the defender; not all defences had to be disclosed at this stage, but only preliminary matters and dilatory exceptions.[34] For *litis contestatio* both parties and their advocates had to take an oath of calumny, that the claim and the defence to it were not malicious or vexatious. Peremptory defences could be raised as matters of fact rather than law, in other words, at a later stage of the trial than formerly.

The trial stage, normally, followed directly before the magistrate who had presided over the pleadings, but a judge delegate (*iudex pedaneus*) might be appointed as a delegate to hear the facts.

From the records of Tiberius Claudius, mayor [of the district] of Pasion, in the ninth year [AD 49] ... from the judgment seat. Pesuris vs. Saraeus [a woman].

Aristocles, advocate for Pesuris: '[Six years ago] Pesuris, for whom I am appearing, took up a child of the masculine sex, Heraclas by name, from the sweepings of the city. He handed him over to his opponent here, and an agreement was made for wet-nursing in the name of Pesuris' son. In the first year she accepted the wages for wet-nursing as agreed. The due day came in the second year, and again she accepted. I speak the truth, for here is her own written acknowledgment of receipt. Pesuris took back the boy when he was weaned. Later, chancing on an opportunity, the wench made her way into the pursuer's house and seized the boy, whom she claims to hold as her son. I have, first, the agreement for wet-nursing, second, the receipt for her fee. I demand submission to the law.'

Saraeus: 'I had already weaned my son when this boy of theirs was handed over to me. I received from them total wages of eight staters. Afterwards the boy died while there were wages outstanding. Now they claim to take from me my own true child.'

Theon: 'We have written documents relating to the little slave boy.'

The mayor of the district: 'Since by his appearance the boy seems to be the son of Saraeus, if she makes, together with

her husband, a written oath about the death of the slave boy
left with her by Pesuris, and if she returns the money she
received, then, in accordance with the decree of the lord
Prefect, it seems to me that she should keep for herself her
own son.'[35]

The same general principles as to discovering the facts seem to
have been observed as in the earlier system, although the witnesses
wanted by the parties were summoned by the court, under penalty,
and interrogated by the judge.

The signatories swear by the Fortune of the Emperor
Antoninus Pius that in good faith they give witness to what is
written below; at the village of Philadelphia in the Arsinoite
territory, in the district of Heraclis, they gave this evidence:
We saw C. Maevius Apella, a veteran of the Aprian cavalry,
beaten with rods and clubs by two constables at the order of
Hierax, mayor of the territory; wherefore in good faith we
are witnesses that we saw him flogged in the village of
Philadelphia. The sixteenth year [AD 153] ... [36]

Documentary evidence, including written depositions, carried
most weight. On the one hand, the rules of evidence had been
clarified and to some extent formalized, for example, on legal
presumptions;[37] on the other hand, the magistrate naturally had a
discretion that a *iudex* appointed to try a specific formula did not.
Judgment by Justinian's time was always given in writing, with
copies for the parties, and also read out in court by the judge.

Execution could also be backed with official power. The
judgment was no longer necessarily limited to money damages;
the court could order the restoration of property, or specific
implement, that is the carrying out of a particular task, such as a
manumission, and the magistrate had the coercive powers to see
this done. Where the judgment was for money, the pursuer still
proceeded against the defender by an action on the judgment.
Execution against the person of the judgment debtor remained
possible (until private prisons were outlawed in or before 486),[38]
but execution against his estate was normal. As time passed, this
ceased to mean a case of universal succession – selling debts and
assets as well as corporeal property, so that it was just as though
the judgment debtor had died – and was replaced simply by
seizure of his property; this would be possessed by court officials

and in due course sold off for the benefit of the creditors.[39] It remained something of a privilege to restrict such seizure to individual items. Where the parties came to a settlement, this was entered in the court records, to avoid any question of the procedural offences, such as prevarication (not pushing a claim) or tergiversation (reneging on a claim), which wasted a court's time even in civil cases.

> The twelfth year [AD 427]. . . . To the chief of the bureau of our most magnificent Prefect of Egypt, . . . , Aurelius Cyrus, son of Leontius, banker of the great city of Alexandria, now living for the pursuit of his business in the famous city of Oxyrhynchus, with the help of Paul the bailiff:
> I approached the aforesaid lord for the granting of a *libellus* or claim when I was raising an action against Nestorius, son of Nestorius, and himself an Alexandrine banker, about monies owed; but since he came and made me satisfaction I have now no dispute with him, nor do I raise nor shall I raise an action on this account. Therefore, having sworn by Almighty God and by the victories of our lords Theodosius and Valentinian, perpetual emperors, I declare that I shall abide by all the aforesaid, nor in any way shall I reverse. And as security I have put into writing this discharge and have given my stipulation.
> Subscription: I, Aurelius Cyrus, son of Leontius (banker in Alexandria) have made a written discharge and have sworn a sacred oath, as is written above.[40]

There was no change in *cognitio* between the Principate and the Dominate, no change, that is, in the sense that the proceedings which had been used in the earlier period continued into the later; there are not two separate types of *cognitio*, although there were many variations. When the formulary system, which had presumably fallen out of use[41] in the course of the later second and early third centuries, was formally abolished in 342,[42] the jurisdiction of the Prefect of the City had already replaced that of the Urban Praetor. However, the constitutional changes and the changes in the sources of law inevitably altered the way *cognitio* functioned in the Dominate. The refined techniques developed by the jurists gave way to a concentration on the substantive law, to the pursuer's rights, as legal technique declined and common sense was meant to supply its want. It is probable that influence

[margin handwritten: abolition of formulary system]

[margin handwritten: Change from focus on procedure to focus on substantive Rs.]

from Hellenistic practice and Christian thought also played some part. Failure to ask for the precise remedy of a particular formula, failure to get niceties right,[43] was no longer fatal, because the discretion of the court enabled it to make reasonable allowances, rather than concentrate on technicalities. These technicalities had been undoubtedly of great help when the formula was first being developed, to provide suitable remedies where the actions in the law had been too general, but they had become outdated. The outdated and unnecessary divisions between the *ius civile* and the *ius honorarium*[44] disappeared from the practice of the courts, although Justinian and the compilers still referred to them.

n b.

APPEAL

Appeal became possible under *cognitio*, whereas the formulary system had only known of *intercessio*, a veto by a tribune, or a magistrate of equal or higher rank than the praetor, of some act done by the Praetor, but this could not apply to the trial before the *iudex*. (This limitation may explain the importance in classical law of the Praetor's power to order *restitutio in integrum*.) The emperor could, of course, use his tribunician veto on the actions of any official, but since most magistrates were in some way or other his delegates there could be appeal from them to him. There is the famous case from Cnidos, where an appeal was made from the city's court to the Emperor Augustus.[45] The emperor appointed a delegate to investigate the facts and on them gave his judgment which was to be registered as the decision of Cnidos:

> Your envoys . . . have appeared before me in Rome and, showing your [city's] judgment, have accused Eubulus, son of Anaxandrides, [Eubulus A] now deceased, and his wife Tryphera, still alive, of the murder of Eubulus, son of Chrysippus [Eubulus C].
> When I requested my friend Asinius Gallus [proconsul of Asia] to question under torture the slaves, who were implicated in the case, I learned that Philinus, son of Chrysippus, had gone for three successive nights to the dwelling of Eubulus A and Tryphera, crying out insults and making a kind of siege; on the third night he took with him his brother Eubulus C. Eubulus A and Tryphera, the owners of the house, since they could neither pacify Philinus nor feel secure in

their home while resisting the siege, ordered one of their slaves, not indeed that he should commit murder, which someone could have inclined to with justifiable rage, but to repel them with the discharge of excrement. However, the slave, whether deliberately or carelessly (he himself denied that he intended it), threw out the chamberpot together with its contents, with the consequence that Eubulus C was fatally injured – who should more properly have been spared than his brother. I have ordered this testimony to be sent to you. I am surprised that the accused so greatly feared your interrogation of their slaves, unless you seemed excessively stern towards the accused and unreasonably severe to those who did indeed, in repelling an outrage, suffer a mischance but in truth did nothing illegal, while you were not angry with those who deserved to suffer all they got, those indeed who three times attacked someone else's house by night, with insults and force, and have undermined the common safety of you all. But now you will visibly satisfy me that you have done rightly when you follow my decision in this matter and enter this letter in your public records.

In *cognitio* appeal was possible from the *iudex pedaneus* to the official who had appointed him, normally the provincial governor, and from him in the Later Empire to the vicar, or else to the Praetorian Prefect; municipal magistrates in Italy appealed to the Urban Praetor. Notice of appeal had to be given within strict time limits, two or three days for the most part, if it was in writing; oral appeal must be made at the time of the sentence. In some circumstances an appeal could be brought by a third party to the judgment; in civil cases, he must have an interest, but in criminal cases 'for humanity's sake' anyone could do so, even if the convicted man objected.[46] The court also must forward the appeal and the dossier within time limits.[47] Appeals could often, until Justinian, be from interlocutory decisions as well as from the final judgment;[48] this could prolong a case almost indefinitely, so Justinian ruled that there could be no more than two appeals in any one case.[49] Frivolous appeals were discouraged by pecuniary penalties, imposed on the litigant or on the judge.[50] Higher courts soon began not merely quashing the decisions of inferior courts, but substituting their own rather than returning the case; they also heard new evidence, and accepted new defences.[51]

In the Principate, when rescripts were still commonly used for settling cases, it was possible for persons to appeal against the emperor as he had expressed himself in a particular rescript: 'if they shall show that what was written in the letter [to the emperor] was false or misrepresented'.[52] Otherwise, of course, it was not possible to appeal from the emperor, nor from the Senate, nor from any judge whom the emperor had appointed to judge on his own behalf, *vice sacra*, and in particular this came in the Later Empire to mean the Praetorian Prefects. Appeal was in general a right, not a privilege; once it was lodged, matters were normally in suspense, but exceptions might be made, for the opening of a will, for example.[53] Again, those classed, for instance, as notorious brigands were not given the right to appeal.[54]

A device was developed to reduce the likelihood of an appeal. An official with jurisdiction might send a letter (*relatio*) to the emperor, together with the dossier of the case, asking for imperial advice on the point of law at issue; this *consultatio* took place before any decision had been given by the court.[55] The replies to these seem to have been the only surviving form of rescript in the later Empire; after Constantine the higher courts might sometimes send in a *consultatio*, even after sentence had been given. Private persons could make a petition (*supplicatio*) to the emperor on the legal issue as long as it had not yet come before a court. The theory was that through such a device the humble would not be intimidated, but it was probably more often used by those of high rank and influence.

Another noticeable feature of the texts on appeal collected in the Digest and the Codes is that they deal with both civil and criminal causes without distinction. This is hardly surprising, in an age when the judge ordinary, the *iudex*, was likely to be the provincial governor, exercising both jurisdictions by virtue of his office.[56] In criminal appeals the appellant might often be released from custody, and in any case his sentence would not be put into effect; this did not apply if he was accepting conviction on major charges and only appealing minor ones.[57] In the Later Empire, however, we find appeal not being allowed at all for certain crimes – the same crimes as those to which amnesties did not apply, that is, homicide, adultery, and the practice of sorcery and magic.[58] The sources, in the sense of what survives to us, are much less rich for criminal than for civil procedure; there is no coherent account. (Moreover, administrative remedies in the sense we know them were to all intents and purposes non-existent.)[59] This can partly be explained by the fact that many of what we in the modern world think of as crimes to be repressed by the state, were to the Romans delicts to be pursued by civil process. Theft was a delict, and so was damage to property (which included slaves), whether deliberate or careless; physical assault upon and defamation of a free person comprised the delict of *iniuria*. The criminal courts must therefore not be imagined as burdened with petty crime. But for serious crimes there were, since the early first century BC, standing jury-courts – *quaestiones perpetuae*. These were replaced in the course of the Principate by officials exercising *cognitio*, in particular at Rome by the Urban Prefect, although the Senate sat regularly as a court for political crimes. In the Later Empire jurisdiction in civil and criminal matters was nearly always concurrent.[60]

NOTES

1 Under Other Sources in ch. 3; see also Arangio-Ruiz (1950); Crook (1994b).

2 Horace *Ep.* 1.16.40–3; cf. Juvenal 8.79–84.

3 Buckland (1939); Watson (1991), 250–65, points out how very different is the stress on procedure in the two systems.

4 *Inst.* 4.6.33e–35; 4.11.2–7; 4.16*pr.*–1.

5 *Inst.* 4.15.8.

6 Kelly (1966a), pp. 6–12; Garnsey (1970), pp. 189ff.; although both are concerned with a later period, the problems must have been much the same.

7 A concurrent jurisdiction might be held by others in some matters, such as that of the curule aediles over the market place.

8 G 4.10–31 is the only coherent description of the procedure, although we have details from others, making up XII T 1–3.

9 G 4.11 – but then so would a charge under the wrong subsection of a Road Traffic Act fall.

10 The actions in the law by the laying on of a hand and by the seizure of a pledge were for enforcement not claim.

11 A real right is a claim to property or something akin to it, such as a servitude; it is a claim that you have a better right to something than does anyone else in the world. A personal right is a claim that a particular person owes you something, because of a contract, a delict, or on some other ground.

12 For a theory, see Kaser (1967). Selb (1984) argues that there was no division until the introduction of (C).

13 As Professor Dieter Nörr has suggested to me.

14 Pliny *Ep.* 6.33.3; Quint. *inst.or.* 12.5.6.

15 But he was here acting as an advocate, rather than a jurist.

16 Gellius 14.2. This was, of course, under the formulary system.

17 Kelly (1966b); Watson (1968); also Mantovani (1992).

18 G 4.30

19 It was therefore always a negative conditional clause, even when it was an appeal to a statute as barring an apparently good claim, e.g. under the Cincian Act restricting gifts over a certain sum to near relatives – but not spouses.

20 For the parts of the formula, see Gaius 4.39–44 & 115ff. & 126–9 & 130–7; also Jolowicz, 203ff.

21 Buckland (1939).

22 See Appendix to ch. 2.

23 Fictions were also used, for example, to allow a foreigner to sue as if he were a Roman citizen, or a slave to be liable – that is, making his owner liable – as if he were a free man.

24 D 1.1.8, Marcian 1 *inst.*

25 In the classical law of marriage, a wife would not normally be in the *familia* of her husband but of her father, or else she would be independent – *sui iuris*; see Robinson (1987).

26 Jolowicz, 398, remarks: 'Indeed one of the roots of the *cognitio* may lie in a distortion of the formulary system by conditions in the provinces.'

27 FIRA iii 167; cf. iii 168.

28 CJ 7.43.1 (Titus) points out that the judge may, but is not compelled to, condemn the contumaciously absent.

29 FIRA iii 169; cf. iii 173 and 175, of the fourth century.

30 Comparable to the earlier *restitutio in integrum.*

31 If he failed in the time allowed he must pay double the defender's costs; he must pay the defender one-tenth of the value of an unsuccessful claim. FIRA iii 168 gives an example of an oath to carry through an action.

32 E.g. FIRA iii 177 of AD 427; cf. CTh 2.14.1, AD 408.

33 de Witt (1926); cf. Pliny *Ep.* 6.33.

34 Dilatory defences were (and are) defences good in themselves, but their use to bar an action can be avoided by a pursuer who delays or adjusts his claim. Peremptory defences are those which bar an action totally; for instance, defences of fraud, illegality, lack of jurisdiction, previous judgment in the same matter.

35 FIRA iii 170. Cf. iii 101 or 172.

36 FIRA iii 188.

37 D 34.3.28.3, Scaevola 16 *dig*; cf. CJ 4.20.1 (undated and unsourced; taken from *Bas.* 21.1.25) & 9, AD 334, & 18, AD 528; *NovJ* 73, AD 538; 90, AD 539.

38 CJ 9.5.1, AD 486; see Robinson (1968).

39 D 42.1.15.2, Ulpian 3 *de off.consulis*; cf. FIRA iii 180.

40 FIRA iii 178; cf. iii 182.

41 But a formula may still have been issued to a *iudex pedaneus* appointed as delegate by a magistrate with *cognitio.*

42 CJ 2.57.1, AD 342.

43 For example, *plus petitio*, as described in Gaius 4.53; reformed in *Inst.* 4.6.33.

44 Already in the late Republic Cicero (*de leg.* 3.3.8) had referred to the Praetor as the guardian of the *ius civile.*

45 FIRA iii 185 = ARS no. 147.
46 D 49.1.4 & 5, Macer 1 *de appell* & Marcian 1 *de appell*; 49.1.6, Ulpian 2 *de appell.*
47 D 49.6.1, Marcian 2 *de appell*; 15 days in CTh 11.30.1, AD 312; 20 days 11.30.8, AD 319; 30 days 11.30.34.1 & 65, AD 364 & 415.
48 E.g. D 49.5.2, Scaevola 4 *reg.* where a court had ordered torture to be used [on a free man] in a civil case, or improperly in a criminal case.
49 CJ 7.70.1, AD 528.
50 CTh 11.36.1 & 2, AD 315.
51 CJ 7.62.6, Diocletian; this has sometimes been thought interpolated – new legislation by Justinian – because of the rulings in CTh 3.30.11, AD 321, or 3.30.52, AD 393.
52 D 49.1.1.1, Ulpian 1 *de appell*, citing Antoninus Pius.
53 D 49.5.7, Paul *de appell.*
54 D 28.3.6.9, Ulpian 10 *ad Sab*; 49.1.16, Modestinus 6 *diff*; cf. PS 5.35.2; CTh 11.36.31, AD 392.
55 E.g. CTh 11.29.2, AD 318.
56 E.g. CTh 2.1.2, AD 355
57 E.g. D 49.7.1, Ulpian 4 *de appell.*
58 CTh 11.36.1, AD 314/15; 11.36.4, AD 339 – this is the enactment which imposes the penalty of the sack on adulterers. Tough on an innocent person wrongfully convicted.
59 Buckland (1937).
60 On all this see Robinson (1995).

Chapter 5

The Uses and Pitfalls of Using the Sources of Roman Law

THE PROBLEMS

We have at least two sets of problems with using the sources[1] of Roman law. One, which can be described in one word – authenticity – has been the concern of lawyers for some five centuries. Its main focus has been and still is on the Digest. Is the law ascribed to the jurists of the classical period really classical? Analogous is the concern with the Codes, the Theodosian Code of AD 438 and Justinian's Code of AD 534. How safely can we accept that the laws attributed to Septimius Severus or Diocletian or Constantine or Julian really are their doing? And the same problem arises even with Gaius, and certainly with *Pauli Sententiae* or the *Collatio*.

The second set of problems is about how far legal sources can be useful for political or social or economic or any other sort of history – other, of course, than legal history! How far do they reflect actuality, what happens in practice, rather than norms, what ought to happen? To describe the law does not describe its working, for example, the constitution of the former USSR guaranteed free speech.

But before we turn to a more detailed consideration of these problems, there is a preliminary difficulty to be faced. What is the Roman law of which we have the sources? And one of the factors that makes the study of Roman law both interesting and difficult, is that it has a later history. Roman law did not come to an end with Justinian's codification in the sixth century. It continued to be of influence through the canon law, and was the source of the great explosion of legal studies which took place in the twelfth century. Including the nineteenth-century codifications, European legal history can be seen as a continuous process of reception or rejection of Roman law. The persistance of its importance may even distort the study of Roman law because romanists know what has continued to influence modern law. This later life does, however, mean that we have no serious problems about the physical survival of the sources in the medieval and modern worlds, other than the usual ones of fire and damp and mice. Since at least twelfth-century Bologna, lawyers have been busy making use of all the Roman sources available; those that have been lost to us almost all disappeared in Roman times or in the post-Roman world called the Dark Ages.

DEFINITIONS

If one talks about 'Roman' law, when does one mean? A portrait of one moment, or at least one period? Or the legal history of Roman law? A modern practising lawyer, in a system such as the South African (and to a lesser extent the Scottish) where Roman law is still a living source, looks to Justinian's codification, and also, perhaps even more, to the commentaries that have been made on it, particularly those of the seventeenth and eighteenth centuries. An academic lawyer, a romanist, looks sometimes at the law of Justinian's time, but more frequently at the Digest, concentrating on the sophisticated law of the classical period, that is from Augustus, or more particularly Hadrian, to the mid-third century. Many classicists are interested in the law of Cicero's day, which is rated by romanists as pre-classical. Historians of the Later Roman Empire concentrate on the Theodosian Code. All of these are Roman law, as are the Twelve Tables of the fifth century BC. But the problems in making use of these different periods of law vary. Some, like Schiller, see post-classical law as a different, and worthless, animal 'completely foreign to the classical law in its evolution, and offering little of value to the student of legal systems on a par with his own'.[2] For him, Justinian's only merit is to have preserved the classical law. Others, such as Buckland or Kaser or Watson, see a coherent if uneven development from the Twelve Tables to Justinian.

The other fundamental problem in the definition of law is, not the period, but the subject matter. The primary definition, to which we have been drawn back over and over again in this book, is the one created by the lawyers, Roman, medieval and modern. It is private law. The great bulk of the sources deals with private law; that was the chief interest of those who wrote or compiled or preserved them. In the Digest sacral law hardly appears; there is one book out of fifty specifically devoted to criminal law (and another to criminalized delicts), and some two can be held to deal with public law. The Codes are more diverse, particularly in that they deal at some length with ecclesiastical and fiscal matters, but private law is still the largest single field treated. Similarly, what has been written about the sources – naturally, mostly by lawyers – has concentrated on private law, both in Roman times and from the twelfth century to the present. This is partly because private law is, in fact, the concern – and the source of income – of most western lawyers, now as then. Then too it is the concern of the propertied classes, those who have the power in and dictate the culture of a society. It is also because private law is the most lawyerly sort of law, the area of, at least relative, legal autonomy. Most ordinary people, however, if asked what they know about law will reply in terms of criminal law.[3] Others, mindful of their social security cheques or children's allowances, might answer in terms of administrative law, even if they did not so phrase it. Politicians might think of constitutional law. A few might remember church law. Thus the weight of the legal sources transmitted to us has a bias that does not correspond to the knowledge or interests of a non-lawyer. The concerns of traditional historians often lead them to concentrate on public law; hence historians and jurists, ancient and modern, can be somewhat at cross-purposes. But historians also know that political and constitutional doctrines have been dragged from legal sources which originally dealt with matters of concern only to individuals.

Private law provides a further problem to the non-lawyer in that, despite superficial appearances, it is not simply a matter of rules, and even rules are often 'soft'. Although a court decision will normally give outright victory to one side or the other, long before that stage is reached there has been a balancing act, balancing rights and duties. Even when people have decided to resort to litigation, a settlement is often reached out of court. It should be remembered that virtually nobody makes a claim in law and that virtually nobody insists on a defence to another's claim, without a conviction of being in the right. For example, suppose a lorry, turning off a main road at a traffic light, which hits a pedestrian crossing the minor road. The pedestrian argues that the signal had only just changed against her, and maintains that the lorry driver was not exercising his duty of care, a duty incumbent on the wielder of such a potent weapon, who should therefore be held liable for any injury or loss she has suffered as a result of the accident. The lorry driver, however, claims that he had a green light and the pedestrian a red one, so he holds that he is not responsible for the accident, not liable to the pedestrian for any damages. The actual injuries to person or property, and the assessment of their value, are factual, not legal matters.

THE AUTHENTICITY OF THE SOURCES

The Digest, as we have said, has been the main focus of argument about authenticity. It was compiled in the early 530s, and consists of extracts from jurists, a few of which go back to the very end of the Republic and most of which were written between three and four centuries before the compilation. These texts were undoubtedly edited by the compilers; the range of alterations made includes excisions, juxtapositions and replacements, as well as additions, but they are all known as interpolations.[4] The search for these interpolations was linked with Humanism, with Faber and Cujas in the sixteenth century, but it was then largely dormant until the nineteenth century. To weigh their importance it seems best to start with the declared aims of the compilation, and the instructions as to its method.

Justinian published with the Digest the enactments he had issued ordering its compilation (*Deo Auctore*), describing his purposes in issuing it (*Omnem*), and confirming its publication (*Tanta*, and the Greek version *Dedoken*). He reasonably remarked that he found the existing sources of law confused and inordinately long. Having completed the (first) Code he wished to present the diverse books of the many jurists in a single volume – a thing never attempted before – and he formed a commission under Tribonian to undertake this. The commission was to read the books written by those to whom the emperors had granted authority to compose and interpret Roman law

> so that the whole substance may be extracted from them, all repetition and discrepancy being as far as possible removed. . . . If you find anything in the old books that is not well expressed, or anything superfluous or wanting in finish, you should get rid of unnecessary prolixity, make up what is

deficient, and present the whole in proportion and in the most elegant form possible. What is more, if you find anything not correctly expressed in the old laws which the ancient writers quoted in their books, you should also take care to rectify it and put it into proper form.[5]

There were to be no contradictions or repetitions, and no overlap with the Code. Any laws which had fallen into desuetude were to be omitted. On publication, the Emperor remarked that he had checked and amended anything that was found to be dubious or uncertain during the drafting of the compilation; all ambiguities had been resolved. The Digest in its fifty books represented only some 5 per cent of what the compilers had read. As ordered, out of reverence for antiquity, the compilers had ascribed to each fragment its author.

All we have done is to provide that if in their legal rulings there seemed to be anything superfluous or imperfect or unsuitable, it should be amplified or curtailed to the requisite extent and be reduced to the most correct form. In many cases of repetition or contradiction, that which appeared to be better has been set down in place of all alternatives and a single authority has been given to the whole, so that whatever has been written there should appear as our own work and composed by our own will. No one may dare to compare any ancient text with that which our authority has introduced, since many very important changes have been made for reasons of practical utility; this has gone so far that where an imperial enactment has been set out in the old books, we have not spared even this but have decided to correct it and revise it in a better form, leaving the names of the ancient authors but preserving by our emendations whatever was proper and necessary to preserve the real intention of the laws in question.

At this stage, the Emperor also admitted that there might be a few cases of repetition, due to human weakness, or because something was relevant in more than one context so that it could not be excluded from some passages without throwing all into confusion.

And in these passages, in which there appeared excellent ideas of the men of old, it would have been thoroughly offensive to split up and separate out something that had been distributed among them piecemeal, as it would have given offence to the minds of readers as well as their ears.[6]

For the same reason, occasional imperial enactments had been allowed into the Digest. He also remarked that not every author read had been included, since in some nothing useful or new had been found.

Justinian thus said that he wanted the whole substance of the jurists selected; further, out of reverence, their names were to be recorded. Their arguments were to be left, even where rejected, so that sense could be made of the whole; this was in implicit contrast to the *Institutes*, which were to be in accordance with contemporary practice and Justinian's own legislation. Moreover, the very project of a collection of juristic writing reveals that the jurists were valued as sources of law separate from the imperial legislation of the past, even although henceforward it was imperial authority which was to give them validity. Why should Justinian have ordered the Digest if he did not want to preserve much of the law of the classical period, more than was likely to have been kept available by the Law of Citations? Furthermore, in the (second) Code, he preserved a style of legislation which had long gone out of use, which must be because he wanted to illustrate how the emperors had exercised authority in the age of the jurists. The secondary, educational, purpose of the Digest would thus be facilitated.

What were the alterations he ordered? Repetitions and inconsistencies were to be removed as were superfluous matters, and when this left a gap it was to be filled, so that the text should read well. This obviously was to be at the discretion of the compilers. If the jurists had made an error about an imperial enactment, this was to be corrected; as we shall see, it had by no means always been easy to discover the existing state of the law or the texts of legislation. What had fallen into desuetude was to be omitted. All of these alterations are relatively minor, even if one can argue that cumulatively they would have a considerable effect. There is no trace of any command to introduce new doctrine, although a revised version of a law might be attributed to a jurist who had not known Justinian's intentions.[7]

During the first half of the twentieth century most leading romanists, led by von Beseler and Albertario, were engaged in interpolation hunting. Their radical criticisms of the texts argued that the Digest gave no picture of classical law, which could only be painfully sought for after all the alterations and accretions of Justinian's compilers, and earlier editors, had been identified and discounted. The attacks began on Tribonian and his colleagues, then switched to the law professors of Beirut and elsewhere in the pre-Justinianic period, and, in the 1930s and 40s, moved to the post-classical editors detected working in the late third and early fourth centuries. Despite the work of Buckland and Riccobono, this fashion only gave way to a more conservative acceptance of the texts some time after World War II; there is a considerable change in attitude in favour of accepting their authenticity between the first and second editions of Kaser's *Das römische Privatrecht.*

The main problem for those who distrust the texts is to identify when such sweeping changes could have been made, when new doctrines would have been introduced. The compilers had a mere three years to read their 3 million lines and creative editing, as opposed to the authorized alterations, would hardly be possible in the time. Some have postulated a pre-Digest, and indeed it seems very likely that there were, in particular areas of law, source books or *florilegia* known to the professors among the compilers, as Schulz pointed out. Nevertheless, Justinian's claim to a task never before attempted makes highly unlikely the existence of any comprehensive collection; he displayed no reluctance in admitting his debt to the codes of Gregorius, Hermogenianus and Theodosius. He also describes in *Tanta* the extent of the work done by the compilers. Justinian's dismissal of the standards of legal education in the past, and his scathing comments on the paucity of books in use do not leave scope for any comprehensive re-editing in the period since the Theodosian Code, a century earlier. The texts were at that time reckoned to be authentic; the Law of Citations makes clear that collation of the manuscripts was expected to produce a reliable text. This, combined with Constantine's confirmation of the classical jurists, argues against any comprehensive reworking of the texts in the immediately post-classical period of Diocletian or later.[8]

The search for interpolations in a fundamental sense depends in fact on a belief that there was a major break in jurisprudence between the classical period and the *Corpus Iuris.* If there is one Roman law, which naturally went through various changes, but which can be traced from the Twelve Tables to the legislation of Justinian, then we avoid the more profound of these difficulties. The presumption is then in favour of the texts being what they allege themselves, subject to the kind of revision that one might expect to find made to books that are used in practice. For these were law-books, not sacred texts, nor was there any copyright. When someone, or some series of people, rewrote Paul or Ulpian to produce a simplified version, it will always have been easier to copy what was there, with omissions of outdated or complicated material, and with linking passages to make sense of the abbreviated version, rather than to invent – just the kind of alteration we find Justinian authorizing. Moreover, it is clear that there were changes within classical law itself, some legislative, others due to a shift in juristic opinion, quite apart from unresolved disagreements. For instance, Hadrian allowed women to make wills without first going through status-loss (*capitis deminutio*); juristic views changed on the acquisition of possession through a free person not in one's power; there remained disagreement as to the age at which a horse became *res mancipi.*

Of course, as was explicit, there were alterations, and it is necessary to be aware of them. Some were simple scribal errors. Others were glosses that crept into a text at some stage; it seems fairly unlikely that Florentinus would have described a memorial monument as 'what the Greeks call a cenotaph'.[9] Then there are Justinianic cross-references, as with the purported sale of something already destroyed, where the compilers harked back to burned houses as well as blown-down trees.[10] Others were deliberate changes to conform with subsequent legislation, such as having Paul accept the rule that a tutor must be 25, a rule due to Justinian himself.[11] Others were omissions of obsolete institutions. For example, the formal conveyance called mancipation and a form of real security which depended on it had disappeared; this kind of real security was called *fiducia* (a feminine noun), but within some texts which talk about real security in the form of *pignus* (a neuter noun) the pronoun *eam* (feminine) appears where *id* (neuter) would have been automatic.[12] Here a grammatical point shows that a change was made, which would not reveal that mancipation had been replaced, because this was by another feminine noun, *traditio.* Generalizations were sometimes made; the Digest statement that the sale of a third party's property was a valid contract, a classical doctrine but at that time taken for granted, was drawn from a text on the validity of sale by a pledge creditor.[13] Juxtaposition of texts from different contexts might be used to round out a doctrine, as with a text of Paul, originally dealing with usucapion but conveniently applied to the law of sale.[14] Hostile references to Christianity in the legal texts must have been excised.[15] Bad Latin or bad logic are really no more likely to be due to the compilers than to the original author.[16] It is necessary to compare texts where we do have parallels, to compare the Digest with PS or PS with Gaius, to compare different versions of the same imperial statute. This has been the great importance of finding independent new fragments, however small.

This general conservatism is not to deny that the law did change, and that new influences affected it. For example, Christianity may have influenced a garbled text on the return of related slaves when a sale was rescinded.[17] But the more serious problem still is the very fact that we only have extracts. We know some views of Alfenus, but we do not know what he thought important nor – necessarily – what was original to him; what we have is what the compilers thought relevant and needing to be said to their audience, and it was they who thought it most aptly said by Alfenus. We know that Ulpian wrote on Sabinus, but how much of the book is Sabinus and how much Ulpian we do not know; moreover, we do not know how much of the somewhat earlier book by Pomponius on Sabinus was used by Ulpian. These difficulties also make the use of computer studies to differentiate between jurists very risky. Further, because the (first) Code was published before the Digest, and the Digest was not to include imperial legislation, we do not know how much law that was almost certainly established by the jurists appears as the fruit of imperial enactments. Our knowledge can never be more than fragmentary, however authentic the individual texts. And always we are the prisoners of the interests of others: what interested the jurists, and how the emperors happened to choose to express themselves, and what, of that, interested the compilers. At least we are not troubled with the problems of correlation between survival and popularity, which seriously affect the literary texts.

The question of authenticity in the Codes is slightly different. Theodosius ordered general legislation from the time of Constantine to be arranged in titles, in chronological order. He accepted that some laws would have to be split among two or more titles. The very words of the enactments were to be preserved as far as they related to essentials. In the original instructions, even superseded laws were to be included, for educational reasons. Future laws issued in one half of the Empire were to receive imperial publication in the other half.[18] Measures were to be taken to ensure that only reliable copies were made for distribution to the provinces. In the interests of brevity and clarity the compilers were to remove superfluous words, add what was necessary, change ambiguities and amend nonsenses.[19] Justinian issued similar instructions for his first Code; the compilers were to remove what was superfluous to the thrust of the law, correct inconsistencies, and omit what was obsolete. The laws were to be arranged, under titles, in chronological order.[20] And for the second Code likewise superfluous, abrogated and inconsistent laws were to be omitted, and the compilers were to present what was valid in elegant form.[21]

It is clear that the emperors wanted authentic texts. But although Theodosius and Justinian desired in general to preserve earlier law, yet these same instructions also allowed for considerable changes of detail, and the exercise of discretion as to what was essential. For instance, Justinian specifically authorized the blending of two or more enactments.[22] All the enactments were shortened; using the Sirmondian Constitutions and occasional parallels in the *Collatio* as a control suggest that excision was more used than paraphrase. But the problem was finding the authentic texts, a task far harder with imperial enactments than juristic writing; we shall shortly look at the issue of the conservation of the sources in the Principate. This was partly a matter of copying accurately; every pre-Theodosian text in Justinian's Code will have been copied from one of the preceding codes, which will have copied it from some 'original' source. The process of legislation had always involved a communication from the emperor to an official, and very often a communication from the recipient to a junior official, and then its publication. Then, the people who wanted to make use of such an enactment normally copied it for themselves. The opportunities for inadvertent corruption of the texts were considerable. Further, it is clear that imperial legislation was not preserved systematically, in one organized central imperial archive. The Theodosian Code itself was to be preserved in the offices of the Praetorian Prefect and of the Urban Prefect, with a third copy to be sent to Africa; another copy was to remain with the constitutionaries who were the officials authorized to licence further copying. How the compilers acquired their texts remains problematic, the more so as we do not know how much of the original Theodosian Code is missing. Matthews has argued that they needed to look widely to find all the valid general constitutions, and that they had to find many in provincial collections, particularly in the West.[23] Sirks holds that they would not have needed to travel much, but could largely draw from the imperial archive, the law schools, and private collections of the nobility.[24] Certainly Justinian's compilers will have had an easier task.

There is also some uncertainty as to the origins of the other pre-Justinianic sources (apart from the Theodosian Code), and the extent to which they were adapted for the conditions of some later period. Again the problem is more serious for those romanists who see the history of Roman law in sharply defined stages rather than as a continuous development. To see classical law ending, just like that, with the death of Ulpian or Modestinus or Severus Alexander, does not fit with the fact that the rescripts of the later third century, up to and including Diocletian, are in the same tradition as their predecessors; lawyers must have still been thinking in the same sort of way.[25] Certainly the cessation of juristic writing will have had an effect; the only source of law now left was the emperor. After a time the traditions of classical law will have become merely a memory, and then one can properly speak of post-classical law. Further, the codes of Gregorius and Hermogenianus produced an authoritative source of rescripts and other imperial enactments.[26] Lawyers probably saw some divergence between juristic writing, conservative in its legal autonomy, and imperial practice, more tuned to react to changing economic and social circumstances.[27] Not that the post-classical authors of this period rejected or even wished to make substantial alterations to the juristic texts, but they did feel the need for some revision, to restore what had become a little out of step. Lawyers will have amended their copies as they used them, since these were manuals for practice, but this does not necessarily mean that the overall nature of the law was changed. And it is changes in detail rather than new doctrines that have been discovered in the group of writings of this period. As to Gaius, arguments have been put forward that the *Institutes* is not a trustworthy classical text, but they have not been generally accepted. De Zulueta wrote in the introduction to his commentary: 'Our own strong impression is that our text is so homogeneous and sustained in character that, apart from *minutiae*, it must be the work of a single author, who can only be Gaius.'[28] As he points out, if Schulz's suggested third-century new edition made no substantial changes, why do we need to posit its existence?

The *Opinions* of Paul was held essentially classical by Mommsen, long before Buckland. Arguments that its omission of reference to the formulary process indicate a mid-fourth century date ignore the fact that *cognitio* was beginning to overtake the formula from the beginning of the Empire, and may well have largely replaced it (except perhaps in Rome) by the end of the second century. It seems likely that the *constitutio Antoniniana* with its universal grant of citizenship within the Roman Empire presupposed a general use of *cognitio*. The formulas published in the Edict could provide a model, rather than a procedural code, for provincial governors and others. The clinching argument for the *Pauli Sententiae* being essentially classical is that Constantine confirmed them along with the other writings of Paul;[29] they must have seemed all of a piece.

The *Epitome* of Ulpian also largely reflects classical law, according to its editor, Schulz, who was willing to see large-scale post-classical editing in other works. Whether or not *Pauli Sententiae* was an anthology, the Vatican Fragments certainly were. They were compiled early in Constantine's reign, since the *damnatio memoriae* of Licinius in AD 324 was not taken into account. Comparison of its juristic texts with passages taken into the Digest show that it retained institutions of the classical law later excised.[30] Again, there is no reason to suppose that its editor did not wish to preserve the classical law, in a suitably selected form, but apart from emendations to individual texts, the process of selection does of itself alter what has been selected. In the absence of new fragments of manuscript, argument is somewhat inclined to be based on prior conceptions as to whether or not there was a break in the continuity of the law. Scholars have argued for extensive interpolation in all these works but, as with the Digest, it seems that the burden of proof should be on the critic.

A related area is the question of the survival of the sources in the Roman world. This is linked with the further question of how accessible the sources were to the Romans themselves. Many Republican *leges* must have been lost or deliberately ignored in the course of the Empire. As we remarked in chapter 2, Cicero alleged there were innumerable statutes on the civil law, and Julius Caesar proposed the publication of an official collection. It seems certain, however, that no such collection was ever made. The jurists and the emperors do not refer to much more than a handful of these statutes, and of some even of these we know nothing.[31] A great part of this disappearance will undoubtedly have been due to policy; most legislation was, and is, political in nature. Many of the private law *leges* will have been overtaken by the legislation of the Principate; others perhaps dealt with details, and such details were better dealt with by jurists, the Senate, or the emperor.

The Senate's records were kept in the *aerarium*, the traditional state treasury, inscribed on wooden tablets, but, apparently, very unsystematically. The publication of the Senate's resolutions seems never to have been a matter of course, although in particular cases the Senate might grant permission for publication, or order steps to be taken to inform the interested parties. These parties, of course, could, and often did, take copies.[32] Again, it seems clear that there was never any comprehensive collection of resolutions of the Senate. Jurists presumably had free access to the archives, but it remains unclear how they were to find what they wanted, assuming they knew it to exist. And the ways they referred to such resolutions were usually vague, not making it easy for a check to be made.[33]

A similar problem existed for imperial legislation in the Principate. Clearly records were preserved, but they were not readily available even to the jurists, let alone the public. Pliny's letters show that even the emperor might not know what his predecessors had issued.[34] In another exchange, Pliny had looked in the provincial archive but had found nothing to the point. Various imperial letters and edicts had been cited to him, but he thought them inaccurate and of doubtful authenticity, so he did not forward them, particularly as he believed that reliable copies would be found in the imperial offices (*in scriniis tuis*). Trajan replied that he had found nothing of general provincial appli- cation in the records (*in commentariis*), although he had found two of the letters cited to Pliny; he agreed that they were not relevant.[35] Indeed, this must have been a real problem – and it explains the need for revisions in the juristic writings, particularly after the production of the *Codex Gregorianus.*

How did the jurists know the positive law if the official records were unsystematic and incomplete? Presumably they trusted the books, the books of their predecessors. Sometimes they must have relied on the memory of what they had participated in, or of what they had been taught.[36] Error could creep in. Before indexing, before the use of the *codex* rather than the roll became common, how available was the law of the past? (Papyrus is relatively fragile, and the format of the roll puts more physical stress on the material than does the *codex*.) And what could officials such as the

Urban Prefect,[37] or provincial governors, or even notaries, know? Obviously carelessness, ignorance, and accident have played their part in the disappearance of formal legal sources, as well as the deliberate discarding of what was seen as no longer relevant. Law-books are kept for use, not for aesthetic reasons, so something clearly obsolete might without much hesitation have been thrown away. On the other hand, law is a conservative discipline, and books, before the modern age of regular new editions, will not readily have been seen as outdated. The later disappearance of the juristic works is explicable. In the West of the Germanic settlements most were too complex and sophisticated to be wanted; it was the simpler manuals which survived. In the East they were of no validity, and therefore of no use, after the publication of the Digest. Moreover, it is undoubtedly true that the energies of copyists from the fourth century onwards were turned towards reproducing Christian works, particularly the Fathers; this is, of course, why some of our legal survivals are palimpsests.

USING THE SOURCES

It does not seem unreasonable to assume that historians are primarily interested in political, administrative or socio-economic matters. Their problem is, how far will they be able to draw on legal sources, directly and indirectly, in these areas? Not only did the Romans have an unwritten constitution, but they seem largely to have taken it for granted. The Republican constitution was built on collegiality and annuality, but it has disappeared from the legal sources as obsolete. There is just one text that is an exception, the fragment of Pomponius' *Enchiridion*, in which he gives an outline of Roman legal and constitutional history.[38] Unfortunately, as we have had occasion to remark in the context of the *ius respondendi*, the fragment is somewhat garbled, and it is not clear how accurate was Pomponius' knowledge. For instance, he writes as though the *legis actio* procedure was logically subsequent to the Twelve Tables, whereas its existence seems assumed in the legislation. His description of the rise of the Senate's power and the authority of its resolutions can only be described as numb and vague. Of the Principate he merely says: 'An emperor was therefore appointed and to him was given the right that what he enacted should be binding'.[39] He holds that the *magistri equitum* of the dictators exercised substantially the same office as the Praetorian Prefects of his day, that is, under the Antonines. The Urban Prefect is described as though his function were still to supervise a festival rather than have the *cura urbis*.[40] Pomponius, however, more than any other single source, does tell us about the jurists, although not necessarily reliably.[41] He remarks that quite a few of Trebatius' books survived, but that they were little read, while those of Labeo were still consulted.[42] He refers to the establishment of the two Schools, the Cassians (more often known as Sabinians) and the Proculians, ascribing their differences to Ateius Capito's conservatism and Labeo's innovatory approach. However, it is very difficult to detect any serious difference of substance between the doctrines of the two Schools, and their very nature remains obscure; it seems more likely that they were aristocratic or mooting clubs rather than having any educational function. Gaius, who was a Sabinian, frequently mentions their disputed points in his *Institutes*; these disputes are also mentioned in the Digest, but by nobody later than Gaius.[43]

Juristic writing in general, unlike that of Cicero, was not much concerned with matters of public law. In the Digest most of Book 1 is concerned with the functions of various magistrates and officials, Book 49 has titles on fiscal and military law, and much of Book 50 is devoted to the functioning of municipalities, but that is some two books out of fifty; nearly all of it comes from the later classical period when jurists had become functionaries. In the Later Empire we find in Justinian's Code that much of Book 1 is devoted to the functions of various officials, and the earlier part to ecclesiastical matters; Book 10 begins with fiscal law and then deals at length with municipalities and local *munera*, which is also the main subject of Book 11. Book 12 is concerned with the structure of the military and civil services; four out of twelve is certainly a much bigger proportion but, as Sirks says in the context of the Theodosian Code,[44] the compilers 'were, as we are not, acquainted with the law in which the rules of the Code were embedded'. The focus of both Digest and Code remained on private law, and on procedure. The Theodosian Code is relatively less concerned with private law. This is partly, as was just said, because of the context of which all lawyers were well aware, and partly because of the definition adopted of 'general' laws, a point to which we shall return.

Obviously much has survived on public law; one has only to consider the majestic works of Marquardt, Mommsen, and de

Martino. But much of this is built up from information in the literary and epigraphic sources. In my own book on the local government law of the City,[45] it is indicative that the index of literary sources is more than twice as long as either of those of legal or epigraphic sources. Information must be trawled for in the legal sources; it is often hidden because it was only incidental to the explicit subject. The legal sources are of no help for the Republican constitution or Republican administration. When we come to the Empire we can see the emperor at work, but there is no analysis of his powers. On the other hand, it would be hard to study the imperial administration without using the legal sources; there they are informative, but as describing what ought to happen, not necessarily what did, as is indeed suggested in the recurrence of laws directed against the wrongdoings of officials.

If the legal sources give relatively little direct information on public law, they give almost none on pagan sacral law. The whole sphere of Roman religion remains a largely sealed book to us, partly because in the Christian Empire efforts were made to wipe all traces away, partly because it was excluded from the Twelve Tables and the whole sphere of law on which the jurists concentrated.[46] On the other hand, there is plenty of material in the two Codes for the ecclesiastical historian. It deals both with doctrine and with the privileges and duties of the clergy, with internal ecclesiastical discipline and with heretics, apostates, Jews, and pagans.

The legal sources give us very little on the economy or financial matters in the public sphere, apart from some state regulation of banking. Nevertheless, when they are combined with the plentiful epigraphic sources and other *negotia*, it is possible to produce a fascinating impression of banking and business life.[47] Not until the crisis of the later third century was there governmental intervention in transactions between private parties, outside the sphere of criminal law; institutions like partnership, save for tax-farmers, were the subject of private law. Diocletian's short-lived Price Edict makes it seem a little more likely that he, not Justinian, was responsible for the two rescripts on *laesio enormis*, in this case, excessively low prices.[48] Taxation is not to be described as intervention, because it merely recognizes an event. There were taxes of various kinds, including *portoria* payable on goods brought into the City;[49] a customs duty was payable at the frontiers of the Empire. There were also taxes on, among other things, inheritances and on the sale of slaves. The rights of the imperial treasury were indeed made the subject of a title in the Digest; the first three fragments are taken (and there is one more short extract) from four books so named written by Callistratus, but nearly all the title is taken from discussions of the private law. Again it is a matter of the legal sources throwing additional light on what we learn from the literary or epigraphic sources.

The social historian can find distinctly more that appears relevant, but must be wary. For all of us in the western (feudal) tradition it is hard to grasp that the Romans had no land law. Land was (in classical law) just one of the *res mancipi*; there were no special forms of conveyance for land, no special kinds of security over it, no special rules about succession to it. Marriage in the Roman world of the late Republic and Principate had as a legal institution almost no content.[50] It had, of course, some consequences, in particular the legal relationship between the father and his children, and also the relationship between husband and wife over the dowry, but there was no regulation of either marriage or divorce. Even when in the Christian Empire a legally causeless or consensual divorce was heavily penalized, it was still valid, because the consenting intention of the parties was essential to marriage. There were, then, different perceptions of the role of the state and the role of the citizen in the functioning of law. For another example, in marked contrast to other slave societies, in particular the American South, there was virtually no law specific to slaves, despite the enormous social and economic importance of slavery; the only real exception concerns manumission, the means by which a slave became a free man. In all other respects in private law, although not in criminal law, the slave could be fitted into the legal treatment of sons, when he was being thought of as a rational being, or the treatment of animals, when he was being thought of as simply property.[51] The historian must hold these two approaches together in any consideration of slavery with legal implications. A related problem here may be that historians expect the law to be a statement of what people must or must not do. Yet much law allows rather than compels. There are rules for making valid wills, yes, but the challenge to a will must nearly always come from a disappointed member of the family; if the family come to a settlement against the wishes of the testator, the courts are most unlikely to become cognizant of it. There is nothing illegal, nothing against the law, in the family agreeing adjustments among themselves, as long as the inheritance tax, the death duties, are paid to the state by someone.

Another problem is that jurists' law is difficult to use, except as anecdotal evidence. Any statistical approach is working with far too many unknowns but, as MacMullen has pointed out,[52] aspirations and fears can also illuminate a society. Worse, such anecdotal evidence may in fact stem from an imaginary case, since the jurists, like the rabbis, argued for intellectual exercise. However, the jurists' imaginary cases were lifelike, unlike the rhetorical exercises of Quintilian and others, which read like fairy-tales.[53] Nevertheless, most juristic law is so abstract, so deliberately remote from the facts except insofar as they were used to pose a question of law, that it is difficult to deduce anything about the flesh and blood social relations from the legal sources alone; the literary and epigraphic (and perhaps the archaeological) sources are also needed for a setting in life.

Further, jurists are primarily concerned with norms, with what ought to happen. Deviance from the norms was not, to jurists, very interesting in itself, although, as remarked in chapter 2, there was some cautelary jurisprudence, trying to foresee difficulties and so taking steps to avoid them. Baker tells us how the Year Books, the early English law reports, recorded the discussion among the serjeants of possible pleas before they committed their words to the record. 'The law was developed, not in decisions upon the known facts of actual cases, but in discussion of supposed facts which could be tried later. . . . The law reporters were not interested in [the] judgments, nor even in trials.'[54] Similarly, what actually happened, how the facts were proved, was of relatively little interest to the Roman jurists; if the correct legal case had been made, then the outcome was of interest only to the parties and its social implications irrelevant. Only occasionally do the jurists seem to have considered the impact of their opinions, and the desirability of achieving a particular result.[55] It is even possible that it was humanity, in view of the result, which led Ulpian to deny the protection of the SC Silanianum to the bona fide possessor or the usufructuary, against the whole rationale of the resolution.[56]

This is linked with the problem of legal autonomy, of how far the law develops on its own terms rather than through social pressures; this is one aspect of legal conservatism. One of the noticeable features of classical Roman law is that it by no means always reflected the social or economic background in the wider world.[57] The jurists often developed law by using the concepts and methods with which they were familiar, even when these were inappropriate. A truly extraordinary example is in the argument over whether barter was sale, when each side adduced a text of Homer to prove the point – and Justinian preserved this.[58] Whatever their perceived picture of the society in which they lived, and its needs as a whole, this was relevant to them as men rather than as jurists.[59] The emperors, on the other hand, were not members of a relatively isolated caste but men with responsibilities demanded of them by explicit popular opinion, from the populace at the games or in debates of the Senate. Consequently, however ineffectively, they do seem to have had the needs of government, often including the needs of their subjects, at heart.

To conclude our concern with private law, there is another reason why a purely legal source will ignore much that is interesting to the historian. Legal sources can only throw indirect light on such questions as the citizen's[60] expectation of justice, on the effectiveness of the technical legal procedures. We have seen how these were supposed to work in chapter 4, but did they? On the one hand there was the network of patronage at all levels of Roman society which could sustain even the humble, but the outcome might depend on whose patron was more in favour at the court of the provincial governor, or the emperor. And even with a patron, a small man must have felt apprehension when involved in a dispute with a great man.[61] There was, however, rudimentary legal aid offered in the Praetor's Edict,[62] and the importance of reputation in Roman society must have often induced submission to due process. The importance of social norms in preserving public order must not be underestimated.[63] One of the features of the Later Empire is the apparent loss of this social cohesion;[64] further, the costs of litigation must have increased very considerably once acting as advocate became a paid profession rather than a social duty. Delays too seem to have become more prevalent, as court structures became more complex, often, ironically, in the hope of achieving better justice. The gap between law in books and law in practice may well have been wider in procedural than in substantive law.

The most fruitful area for the historian is probably the study of criminal law; here the legal sources are the obvious place to start. Books 47 and 48 of the Digest are concerned with criminalized delicts and with the crimes of the *ordo*, as is Book 9 in each of the two Codes. We are told about individual crimes and also about accusations and the custody of those accused, about interrogation under torture and punishments. There is no abstract discussion of the definition of crime or of criminal liability, although these can be deduced from the texts. There is, of course, no consideration of such things as how often the law was broken, how frequently an accusation was made, how reliable were convictions, and what penalties were actually imposed, but then, none of these things would be found in a modern textbook. For such a viewpoint, we must turn to the literary sources. The enactments in the Codes inform us of what the emperor wished to repress, whether of his own initiative or under pressure from some interested person or group, and whether he felt strongly enough to threaten lurid punishment.

This is probably a suitable point to consider why, particularly in the Later Empire, emperors repeatedly re-enacted the same, or nearly the same, laws. Partly this was because legislation had a rather different function in the Roman world; we shall discuss legislation as ideology in the next paragraph, before going on to discuss some of the legislative peculiarities of the Theodosian Code. But it also reflected a need we have in the modern world to re-enact legislation against prevalent crime as offenders, or their lawyers, discover new loopholes. Where the consequences of being mistaken as to the law might be very serious, 'reiterated requests for clarification indicate the eagerness of subjects and *iudices* to be accurately informed in cases of doubt'.[65] Then, in a world without mass communication – except insofar as coinage fulfilled this role – it might be desirable to stress that a new emperor wished to follow the policies of his predecessor, or laws might be repeated just for emphasis. As Pliny's correspondence shows, a law published in one province did not necessarily have validity in another.[66] And a further reason for issuing a law was probably that it showed that something was being done, that people's problems were recognized, that they were not forsaken by their emperor. The repetition of legislation in the Later Empire seems explicable enough, and the preservation of it is because these were general laws, and they had not been abrogated.

This brings us to the ideology of legislation. The non-lawyer is likely to see law in terms of legislation, and legislation as something objective and factual. This may have been relatively true in the later Republic and Principate, when *leges* do not read so very differently from modern legislation. The Twelve Tables too settled certain limited issues, after a political struggle; they were not a general code, any more than Magna Carta. Law is more than legislation, as the description of the sources in chapter 2 should have made clear, and law is more than rules; it is also an ordering of rules, a way of seeing their inter-relationships, and of creating priorities. In the Later Empire legislation was easily the most important manifestation of law, and it was undoubtedly used as propaganda. The emperors wanted to pass on a message, a message phrased in norms, but related more to the moral climate desired than to administrative needs. For example, there was the enactment against those who troubled the spirits of the dead by sorcery, with the sanction: 'let a pestilence carry him off'.[67] Those to whom the law was addressed were to recognize the horror that sorcery should induce. The language used was indeed meant to communicate, but to communicate power and remoteness, awe and authority. An emperor was expected to use a high style when speaking to the whole people or to high officials; the style of the rescripts was suitable for the common man.[68] Legislation was more to be used than admired, certainly, when compared with rhetoric or literature; however, unless it was admirable by the canons of rhetoric and literature it would have less force, be less usable. Thus we find in the Codes law that seems hardly recognizable to modern ears, but which could be interpreted reliably by those to whom it was addressed, who shared in the culture of the time, and who were administrators as much as lawyers. As Honoré has said of the Theodosian Code: 'Its content is legal in the sense that it consists of the operative parts of laws enacted by Roman emperors, but the expression of these laws is not what a lawyer would expect'.[69]

In obedience to the command to collect all the laws since Constantine resting 'upon the force of edicts or sacred imperial law of general force', the compilers included some rather strange provisions in the Theodosian Code. There is, for instance, the entirely hygienic command that horses should be washed downstream of army encampments.[70] There is also an almost incoherently hysterical invitation to accuse senior officials:[71]

If there is any person of any position, rank or dignity whatever who believes that he is able to prove anything truthfully and clearly against any judge, count, or any of My retainers or palatines, in that any of these persons has committed some act which appears to have been done without integrity and justice, let him approach Me and appeal to Me unafraid and secure. I Myself will hear everything; I Myself will conduct an investigation; and if the charge should be proved I Myself will avenge Myself. Let him speak with safety, and let him speak with a clear conscience. If he should prove the case, as I have said, I Myself will avenge Myself on that person who has deceived Me up to this time with feigned integrity. The person, moreover, who has revealed and proved the offence I will enrich with honours as well as with material rewards. Thus may the Highest Divinity always be propitious to Me and keep Me unharmed, as I hope, with the State most happy and flourishing.

Thus what they collected was not always lawyers' law, but they took literally what the emperor had said was to take effect for all time. They were themselves lawyers, who had also available to them the legislation collected in the Gregorian and Hermogenian Codes, and the Law of Citations to give them a guide to reliable juristic writing. This uncritical acceptance of 'general' laws is what has made lawyers often feel unhappy with a code so difficult to administer, but it is also the main reason why the Theodosian Code, rather than Justinian's, has been such a happy hunting ground for historians of the Later Empire.

We have touched on law in books vs. law in practice in connection with the citizen's chances of justice, but the problem needs further consideration. Did ordinary people use the kind of law described by Gaius? The picture we can draw, which looks at first sight so full of detail (as illustrated in FIRA iii), when taken over the centuries and over the physical extent of the Empire, is sketchy indeed; a modern sociological lawyer would be baffled by the lack of statistically valid data.[72] Nevertheless, if the evidence points in the same general direction, it does not seem unreasonable to draw tentative conclusions. Law, private law, is there to regulate the conduct of the citizens between each other; we do not always have to worry about status inequality. We have referred in chapter 3 to some of the *negotia* which have survived and, not entirely surprisingly, we have seen a mixed picture of observance of the details of the learned law. But Roman law was, until the third century, essentially the law of Rome and Italy; if we confine ourselves to this area, we find in general a close observance of the norms to be found in Gaius. For example, at Herculaneum, the literal (or written) contract, about which we know little from the sources mediated through Justinian, was flourishing. It was not always quite as simple as Gaius' account makes out, because men of business were concerned with questions of proof as much as the constitution of an obligation, but it was in regular use for the novation of a debt along a chain of creditors.[73] At Puteoli, the wax tablets of the Sulpicii have shown that 'Roman private law in the Julio-Claudian age was not just a professional mystique. The precision and formality with which these documents were drafted . . . shows that it was assumed by the businessmen of Puteoli that the full range and subtlety of the jurist-made system applied to their affairs.'[74]

The literary evidence that we have for a more casual attitude is largely concerned with family matters. As we have said concerning the law of wills, and as was also true of the law of adultery,[75] it was in these more private, familial areas that the actual will of the parties was more important than the default standards laid down by the law. In all Cicero's letters we never learn who was his wife's tutor; we find him, despite the theoretically almost unlimited powers of the *paterfamilias*, helpless before Tullia's marriage to Dolabella. Pliny's letters record, with varying degrees of approval, a number of women making wills with no mention of status loss, which was requisite until a SC of the reign of Hadrian; this implies it was either so trivial or so regular a ritual that it was not worth mentioning. He twice mentions an emancipation; both were in order that someone could be an heir when the testator would not have left his estate to the *paterfamilias*. Regulus released his son in order that the boy could inherit his mother's estate.[76] In the other, strange, case a man took a violent dislike to his son-in-law but made his granddaughter by him his heir on condition that she was released from her father's power; she was released by her father but only to be adopted by her father's brother.[77] Nevertheless, the overall impression is that there was not a great gap, although there was not an exact coincidence, between law in books and law in practice.

We can move this argument to a different stage. How reliable are literary descriptions of law in practice? There are two cases where we have a legal and a historical source for the same episode. In 186 BC there was a major scandal at Rome concerned with the cult of Bacchus.[78] We have an inscription recording the resolution of the

Senate passed to deal with the case. The cult was forbidden, but if it was obligatory on someone to belong to it, application was to be made to the Urban Praetor; a quorum of 100 senators was needed to approve this, and the other details. No male was to be a member, not even as priest or president, and indeed there was to be no president, no common funds, no magistrate or deputy. There was to be no coming together to swear any form of oath. Practice of the cult was not to be secret nor practised outside Rome without the approval of the Praetor. No meeting of the cult was to consist of more than five persons – no more than two men, no more than three women – except with the authorization of the Praetor. These regulations were to be publicly proclaimed over a period of at least three market days. The penalty for breach of them was capital, and any other existing groups were to disperse within ten days. This resolution of the Senate is concerned only with the measures to be taken; naturally it does not talk about the genesis of the affair. Livy devotes twelve chapters (and some further passages) to the scandalous crime; his language is a little more moderate than that of the gutter press, but he is concerned to produce much of the same Shock! Horror! effect from a story full of sex and unnameable crimes and midnight orgies, and involving senatorial ladies at that. On the other hand, his description of the Senate's resolution is:

> that there should be no Bacchanalia in Rome or Italy. If any person considered such worship to be ordained by tradition or to be necessary, and believed that he could not omit it without sin and atonement, he was to make a declaration before the Urban Praetor, and the latter would consult the Senate. If permission were granted to him, at a meeting where not fewer than 100 were in attendance, he should offer the sacrifice, provided that not more than five people should take part in the rite, and that there should be no common purse or master of sacrifices or priest.[79]

Whether or not Livy had actually seen a copy of the resolution of the Senate, he transmitted at least part of its contents quite accurately. In this case we should find the inscription, although giving the text of legislation of a sort, rather meagre without the literary expansion, even though the bias from which Livy tells the story raises its own difficulties.[80]

The other case is the adlection – direct admission – into

the Senate by the Emperor Claudius of certain nobles of the Gauls.[81] Claudius had this speech engraved in bronze; its exact constitutional status is unclear, partly because the opening part is missing, but it clearly stemmed from his authority as censor. The proposal was a novelty. Tiberius had admitted to the Senate provincials from the colonies and municipalities of the Empire, but their acceptance seems to have been based on their being the leading men of these cities, just like those prominent in the Italian towns; Claudius was proposing to grant this privilege to wealthy and powerful young men who were technically tribal chiefs. This process of romanization was clarified by his shortly afterwards granting municipal rights to certain Gallic towns, a policy continued by Nero. Tacitus implies that Claudius was opening Rome to the barbarians; such opposition was perhaps not very surprising, but it was an attitude which could only have been taken by the same kind of 'insiders' as we considered in the context of the *ius respondendi*. Moreover, Tacitus' version of the actual speech is more concerned with citizenship than the Senate; it is its context in the *Annals* which makes clear the issue. As was said long ago:

> If, when the speech was the emperor's, fully preserved, carefully arranged, and dealing with a matter of intense interest to the senatorial order, [Tacitus] chose to insert what was practically a composition of his own, still less in other cases . . . can we reasonably look in Tacitus for general résumés of other speeches.[82]

However, he does tell us that the Senate resolved to accept Claudius' proposal, and that certain of the Aedui were admitted as part of a general censorial review of the Senate. Here the force of the emperor's *oratio* is debatable, but it must be treated as a source of law at least at the level of a censor's edict – and one not liable to veto at that. But the episode shows that Tacitus was prone to be economical with the truth.

Questions remain about the sources of law, and their use in the twentieth century, by lawyers as well as historians. Roman law as a whole remains a source, even if only a historic source, in some systems, such as the South African and the Scottish. But there are questions, especially for the classical law, that tantalize the legal historian. How precisely should a jurist be defined?[83] Clearly he was a member of the upper classes. The notary, the useful little man who had a book of forms and styles, and had his shingle on the corner of the street, was not classed as a jurist. How many jurists were there ever? How many were counted as jurists at one time? Was there a feeling that there should be no more than half a dozen or a dozen, or was it simply a matter of peer recognition among the aristocracy? In what relationship to the jurists did provincial advocates who practised before the governor stand? Had they sometimes, or often, spent time in Rome, listening to the jurists or attending the *stationes* referred to by Aulus Gellius? How early was there a profession of notaries, and can we trace their history unbroken into the medieval world?[84]

I should like to finish with an illustration of what to a romanist seems an appalling example of the cross-purposes at which scholars, engaged in broadly the same field, can find themselves. As a legal historian I consider that a major part of the pagan literature surviving from antiquity is the Digest, and the pre-Justinianic legal sources. But in a relatively recent book on texts and their transmission[85] only Gaius is mentioned of all the legal sources (in the chapter 2 sense); this is presumably because the author decided to take Apuleius as his terminus. But, in view of the massive size of the Digest – roughly one and a half times the length of the Bible – why did he choose Apuleius as the end of pagan literary culture? If a legal work is not 'literary' he should not have included Gaius. Literally the only other references to legal texts in this book are to refer to them as secular works of a technical nature (Intro. p. xvi) without any more description, and then to mention in a footnote on p. xviii that manuscripts of CTh and LRV [sic] were copied at Lyon. So a philologist can ignore the most influential fruit of secular Roman culture, while discussing obscure poets . . . . Certainly we are at cross-purposes. I do not deny that literature is necessary for the civilized life, but so is law. Is the author quite unaware that the intellectual excitement caused in medieval Europe by Irnerius and the Four Doctors at Bologna – and Gratian too – was as profound as, and even more influential than, that of Abelard and theology in Paris, let alone any poet?

NOTES

1 In this chapter sources normally means those which were described in ch. 3, the sources as we have them transmitted to us, including the *negotia*.

2 Schiller (1978), p. 586.

3 I have more than once been asked, when representing 'law' at careers conventions for school-children, about the police force.

4 There is a huge literature; there is even an *Index Interpolationum*. However, it dates from a period when radical criticism was all the fashion, that is, the view that our sources were heavily altered, and in doctrine as well as vocabulary.

5 *Deo Auctore* 4 & 7.

6 *Tanta pr.* & 1 & 10 & 11 & 13(14) & 14 & 17.

7 Watson (1994) points out that all substantive interpolations are either where we know that Justinian legislated, as evidenced in the Code, or where, of two functionally related classical institutions, one disappeared and the other was used to patch the gap.

8 CTh 1.4.3, AD 426; 1.4.2, AD 327/8.

9 D 11.7.42, Florentinus 7 *inst.*

10 D 18.1.58, Papinian 10 *quaest*, made to refer to the preceding fragment, by the later jurist Paul.

11 D 26.2.32.2, Paul 9 *resp*; CJ 5.30.5, AD 529.

12 D 13.7.8.3, Pomponius 35 *ad Sab.*

13 D 18.1.28, Ulpian 41 *ad Sab*; see Daube (1952).

14 D 18.1.52, Paul 54 *ad ed*; see Daube (1957), where he also points out, at pp. 617–18 of his *Collected Studies* (Frankfurt, 1991), a (classical) grammatical error and a scribal error.

15 Lactantius (*div.inst.* 5.11.19) tells us that persecuting rescripts had been collected by Ulpian in 7 *de off.proconsulis.*

16 D 21.1.11, Paul 11 *ad Sab* is not logical, but its classicality is confirmed by Gellius 4.2.12. Lawyers' use of language is by no means always elegant.

17 D 21.1.35, Ulpian 1 *ad ed.aed.cur*; see Buckland (1941). It is possible that Ulpian had humane inclinations; see infra p. 119, fn. 57.

18 CTh *Gesta Senatus* 4, AD 429; cf. CTh 1.1.5, AD 429.

19 CTh 1.1.6, AD 435. One cannot but wonder about their ideas of brevity and clarity.

20 CJ *c. Haec quae necessario* 2.

21 CJ *c. Cordi* 3.

22 *Haec quae necessario* 2; e.g. CJ 9.36.2 , AD 365, which uses CTh 9.34.7, AD ?365, & 9, AD 386; cf. CJ 9.49.9, AD 396, using CTh 9.42.15, AD 396, & 1, AD 321.

23 Matthews (1993), at pp. 31–44.

24 Sirks (1993). He points out that the problems of reconciling confused dating has no direct relevance to the authenticity of the texts.

25 Watson (1973).

26 Wolff (1949), especially at p. 84.

27 Watson (1974b).

28 de Zulueta (1953) at p. 6. As someone who has also translated Gaius for publication, I can only say that I agree wholeheartedly; it is one man's work, and it consists of, or is based on, lecture notes.

29 CTh 1.4.2, AD 327/8.

30 Perhaps most notably FV 1 contrasted with D 18.1.27, Paul 8 *ad Sab.*

31 E.g. D 11.5.3, Marcian 5 *reg.*

32 E.g. FIRA i 47 – 'descriptum et recognitum ex libro sententiarum in senatu dictarum'.

33 Talbert (1984), at pp. 304–5; he cites the exchange between Trajan

and Pliny (*Ep.* 10.72–3) where the emperor wanted Pliny to send him the Senate's resolution.

34 Pliny *Ep.* 10.58; 10.79. In both cases Pliny sent copies of imperial *epistulae* and edicts to Trajan; cf. FIRA i 82.

35 Pliny *Ep.* 10.65–6.

36 There were law schools of some sort in the second century, for Gellius mentions (13.13) 'stationes ius publice docentium aut respondentium'; for later establishments, see Liebs (1987).

37 Symmachus, Prefect of Rome in AD 384, seems to have confined himself to recent legislation.

38 D 1.2.2; it takes up seven columns of the stereotype.

39 D 1.2.2.6 & 9 & 11, Pomponius *enchir.*

40 D 1.2.2.19 & 33, *ibid.*

41 Schulz (1953) p. 46ff.

42 D 1.2.2.42 & 45 & 47, *ibid.*

43 D 1.2.2.47–8 & 51–3, *ibid;* see also Jolowicz, 378–80; Schiller (1978), 327–30.

44 Sirks (1993), at p. 63.

45 Robinson (1994).

46 See, above all, Watson (1992).

47 Andreau (1987).

48 CJ 4.44.2 & 8, AD 285 & 293.

49 Palmer (1980).

50 A woman's status did not change because she was married; she was either in her father's power or independent of paternal power. Her becoming a threefold mother did however release her from tutory, but tutory was not power, and her husband had no right even of tutory.

51 Watson (1987).

52 MacMullen (1980).

53 Crook (1967) at p. 15.

54 Baker (1979) at pp. 69–70; cf. Cicero, *Topica* 11.50–12.51.

55 See D 21.2.31, Ulpian 42 *ad Sab,* and 17.1.6.6, Ulpian 31 *ad ed,* discussed in Watson (1995) at p. 86f. and p. 104ff.; cf. Watson (1972b).

56 D 29.5.1.2, Ulpian 50 *ad ed.*

57 *Inst.* 2.14*pr.* shows Justinian as a real reformer; cf. D 45.3.9.1, Ulpian 48 *ad Sab,* where the answer is obviously unsatisfactory for slave owners. D 16.3.1.5, Ulpian 30 *ad ed,* produces a bizarre result; see Watson (1995) p. 89. See too Watson (1976).

58 D 18.1.1.1, Paul 33 *ad ed;* cf. G 3.141; *Inst.* 3.23.2.

59 Watson (1992), esp. ch. 10.

60 The term 'citizen' is used to cover the likely parties to litigation; it must therefore, in this sort of context, be extended to include not only peregrines on occasion, but more frequently the slaves of citizens.

61 Kelly (1966a).

62 Praetor's Edict 14: 'Si non habebunt advocatum, ego dabo', from D 3.1.1.4, Ulpian 6 *ad ed.*

63 MacMullen (1980); Nippel (1995).

64 MacMullen (1988).

65 Harries & Wood (1993) at p. 15.

66 Incidentally, no jurist seems ever to have made use of Pliny's Book 10 as a source for provincial *epistulae* or mandates.

67 CTh 9.16.5, AD 357.

68 Rescripts were anyway restricted to the instant case by Arcadius and Honorius – CTh 1.2.11, AD 398; cf. CJ 1.14.2, AD 426. On Roman bureaucratese, see MacMullen (1960).

69 Honoré (1986).

70 CTh 7.1.13, AD 391.

71 CTh 9.1.4, AD 325.

72 Efforts have been made by such historians as Keith Hopkins and R.P.Duncan-Jones in the fields of sociology and economics.

73 Arangio-Ruiz (1950); cf. Andreau (1974).

74 Crook (1994b) reviewing Camodeca (1992).

75 Robinson (1996).

76 Pliny *Ep.* 4.2.

77 Pliny *Ep.* 8.18. Pliny appears to be describing the correct legal process: '... si esset manu patris emissa. Emiserat pater adoptaverat patruus ...'. She could almost certainly not at this period have been first emancipated and then adopted, but Pliny, nevertheless, speaks of her later in the sentence as 'emancipatam'; this is probably careless language rather than bad law.

78 Livy 39.8–19; FIRA i 30 = ARS no. 28; see also Pailler (1988).

79 Livy 39.18.

80 Bauman (1990).

81 Tacitus *Annals* 11.23–5; FIRA i 43 = ARS no. 129.

82 Hardy (1912) at p. 146.

83 Cf. Cicero *ad fam.* 7.21; cf. *pro Balbo* 20.45 for specialist lawyers who did not count as jurists.

84 Teitler (1985); Schulz (1953) at p. 155.

85 *Texts and Transmission*, ed. L.D.Reynolds (Oxford University Press, 1983)

Further Reading

This is by no means a complete Bibliography, but a mixture of suggested further reading and a list of the works referred to in the text.

Andreau, J. (1974) *Les affaires de Monsieur Jucundus*, Rome, École Française
—— (1987) *La vie financière dans le monde romain*, Rome, Bulletin École Française à Rome
Arangio-Ruiz, V. (1934) 'Les nouveaux fragments des *Institutes* de Gaius', repr. (Jovene, Camerino, 1977) in *Scritti di Diritto Romano* III, 1–24
—— (1935) 42 *BIDR*, 570–624, 'Il nuovo Gaio: discussioni e revisioni'
—— (1948a) 1 *RIDA*, 9–25, 'Les tablettes d'Herculaneum'
—— (1948b) 3 *PP*, 129–51, 'Processo di Giusta'
—— (1950) *Atti Modena*, repr. in *Studi Epigrafici e Papirologici* (Naples, 1974), 355–62, 'Le tavolette cerate ercolanesi e il contratto letterale'
—— (1951) 6 *PP*, 116–23, Nuove osservazioni sul processo di Giusta'
—— (1959) 62/1^{3s} *BIDR*, 223–45, 'Tavolette ercolanesi: il processo di Giusta'
—— (1974) *Studi Epigrafici e Papirologici*, Naples
Archi, G.G., M. David et al. (1956) *Studia Gaiana* IV: *Pauli Sententiarum: fragmentum Leidense*, Leiden
Bagnall, R.S. (1995) *Reading Papyri, Writing Ancient History*, Routledge, London
Bahn, P.G. (1992) 45 *Archaeology*, 60–5, 'Letters from a Roman garrison'

Baker, J.H. (1979, 2nd edn) *An Introduction to English Legal History*, Butterworth, London

Bandy, A.C. (1983) see Lydus, Johannes

Bauman, R.A. (1974) 33 *Latomus*, 245–64, 'Criminal prosecution by the aediles'

—— (1985) *Lawyers in Roman transitional politics*, Munich

—— (1990) 39 *Historia*, 334–48, 'The suppression of the Bacchanals: five questions'

—— (1995) 112 *SZ*, 385–99, 'The death of Ulpian, the irresistible force and the immovable object'

Behrends, O., R.Knütel, B.Kupisch & H.H.Seiler (eds) (1990–) *Corpus Iuris Civilis: Text und Übersetzung*, Heidelberg

Berger, A. (1953) *Encyclopedic Dictionary of Roman Law*, APS, Pennsylvania

Birks, P.B.H. & G.MacLeod (trs) (1987) *The Institutions of Justinian*, Duckworth, London

Bleicken, J. (1962) *Senatsgericht und Kaisergericht*, Göttingen

Bluhme, F. (1820) 4 *ZS für geschichtliche Rechtswissenschaft*, 257–472, 'Die Ordnung der Fragmente in den Pandectentiteln'

Böcking, E. et al. (1837–44) *Corpus Iuris Romani Anteiustiniani*, Bonn, repr. 1987, Aalen, Scientia

Bonfante, P., C.Fadda, C.Ferrini, S.Riccobono & V.Scialoja (1960) *Digesta Iustiniani Augusti*, Milan

Borkowski, A. (1994) *A Textbook on Roman Law*, Blackstone, London

Bowman, Alan K. & J.David Thomas (1983) *Britannia* Monograph 4: *Vindolanda: the Latin Writing-Tablets*

—— (1986) 76 *JRS*, 120–3, 'Vindolanda 1985: the new writing tablets'

—— (1991) 81 *JRS*, 62–73, 'A military strength report from Vindolanda'

Bruns, C.G. (1909) *Fontes iuris romani antiqui*, Tübingen, 7th edn by O.Gradenwitz, repr. 1956

Bruun, C. (1991) *The Water Supply of Ancient Rome*, Helsinki

Buckland, W.W. (1924) 33 *Yale LJ*, 343–64, 'Interpolations in the Digest'

—— (1930) 10 *TR*, 117–42, 'D 47.2 *de furtis* and the methods of the compilers'

—— (1934) 13^{4s} *RHD*, 81–96, 'L'*edictum provinciale*'

—— (1936) 48 *JR*, 339–64, 'Reflections suggested by the new fragments of Gaius'

—— (1937) 27 *JRS*, 37–47, 'Civil proceedings against ex-magistrates in the Republic'

—— (1939) 13 *Tul.LR*, 163–77, 'Praetor and Chancellor'

—— (1941) 54 *HLR*, 1273–1310, 'Interpolations in the Digest: a criticism of criticism'

—— (1944) 60 *LQR*, 361–5, 'The *interpretationes* to PS and the *Codex Theodosianus*'

—— (1945) 61 *LQR*, 34–48, 'PS and the compilers of the Digest'

—— (1963, 3rd edn revised P.Stein) *A Textbook of Roman Law from Augustus to Justinian*, Cambridge University Press

Caimi, J. (1984) *Burocrazia e diritto nel de magistratibus di Giovanni Lido*, Milan

Cameron, A. (1993) *The Mediterranean World in Late Antiquity* AD 395–600, Routledge, London

Camodeca, G. (1992) *L'Archivio Puteolano dei Sulpicii*, Naples

Cary, M. (1929) 19 *JRS*, 113–19, 'Notes on the legislation of Julius Caesar'

Ciulei, G. (1983) *Les tryptiques de Transylvanie: études juridiques*, Zutphen

Coleman, K.M. (1990) 80 *JRS*, 44–73, 'Fatal charades: Roman executions staged as mythological enactments'

Costa, E. (1927, 2nd edn) *Cicerone giurisconsulto*, Bologna

Crawford, M.H. (1974) *Roman Republican Coinage*, Cambridge University Press

—— (1985) *Coinage and Money under the Roman Republic*, London

—— (1995) *Roman Statutes*, London, BICS Supp. 64 [= Roman Statutes]

Croke, B. (1983) 13 *Chiron*, 81–119, 'The manufacture of a turning point'

—— (1993) 'Mommsen's encounter with the Code', 217–39, in J.Harries & I.Wood (eds) *The Theodosian Code: Studies in the Imperial Law of Late Antiquity*, Duckworth, London

Crook, J.A. (1955) *Consilium principis*, Cambridge University Press

—— (1967) *Law and Life of Rome*, Thames & Hudson, London

—— (1994a) *CAH* IX^2, 531–63, ch. 14: 'The development of Roman private law'

—— (1994b) 84 *JRS*, 260–1, review of Camodeca (1992)

D'Arms, J.H. & E.C.Kopff (eds) (1980) *The Seaborne Commerce of Ancient Rome*, American Academy, Rome

Daube, D. (1951) 41 *JRS*, 66–70, 'The peregrine praetor'

—— (1952) *St. Arangio-Ruiz* I, 185–200, 'Generalisations in D 18.1, *de contrahenda emptione*'

—— (1957) 73 *LQR*, 379–98, 'Three notes on D 18.1, conclusion of sale'

✓ —— (1961) 3 *Jewish J. of Sociology*, 3–28, 'Texts and interpretation in Roman and Jewish law'

David, M. & H.L.W.Nelson (1955) 23 *TR*, 75–82, 'Das neue Leidener Paulus-Fragment'

Dessau, see ILS

de Witt, N. (1926) 21 *CP*, 218–24, 'Litigation in the Forum in Cicero's time'

de Zulueta, F. (1928) 44 *LQR*, 198–205, 'The Oxyrhynchus Gaius'

—— (1934–36) 24–26 *JRS*, 168–86 & 19–32 & 174–86, 'The new fragments of Gaius'

—— (1946) *The Institutes of Gaius*, vol. I, *Text with critical notes and translation*, Oxford University Press

—— (1953) *The Institutes of Gaius*, vol. II, *Commentary*, Oxford University Press

Digest, see O.Behrends et al;
   P.Bonfante et al;
   A.Watson (1985)

Dirksen, H.E. (1824) *Übersicht der bisherigen Versuche zur Kritik und Herstellung des Textes der Zwölf-Tafel-Fragmente*, Leipzig

Dittenberger, W., see SIG

Duckworth, G.E. (1952, with additions 1994, Bristol Classical Press) *The Nature of Roman Comedy*, Princeton University Press

Francisci, P. de (1922) 3 *Aegyptus*, 68–79, 'Frammento di un indice del primo Codice Giustinianeo'

Frier, B.W. (1980) *Landlords and Tenants in Imperial Rome*, Princeton University Press

Galsterer, H. (1988) 78 *JRS*, 78–90, '*Municipium Flavium Irnitanum*'

Gardner, J.F. (1996) 42 *Labeo*, 83–100, 'Hadrian and the social legacy of Augustus'

Garnsey, P. (1970) *Social Status and Legal Privilege*, Oxford University Press

Gaudemet, J. (1979, 2nd edn) *La formation du droit séculier et du droit de l'Église aux IVe et Ve siècles*, Paris

—— (1982, 2nd edn) *Institutions de l'antiquité*, Paris

Girard, see *Textes*

Gonzalez, J. (1986) 76 *JRS*, 147–243, 'The *lex Irnitana*: a new copy of the Flavian municipal law'

Gordon, W.M. (1994) 'Going to the fair – Jacques de Révigny on possession', 73–97 in A.D.E.Lewis & D.J.Ibbetson (eds) *The Roman Law Tradition*, Cambridge University Press

Gordon, W.M. & O.F.Robinson (trs) (1988) *The Institutes of Gaius*, Duckworth, London

Greenidge, A.H.J. (1901) *The Legal Procedure of Cicero's Time*, Oxford University Press

Grierson, P. (1956) *Essays in Roman Coinage presented to H.Mattingly*, 240–61, 'The Roman law of counterfeiting'

Gualandi, G. (1963) *Legislazione imperiale e giurisprudenza*, Milan

Haenel, G.F. (1849) *Lex Romana Visigothorum*, Leipzig, repr. Aalen, Scientia, 1962

Harries, J. (1988) 78 *JRS*, 148–72, 'The Roman imperial quaestor from Constantine to Theodosius II'

Harries, J & I.Wood (eds) (1993) *The Theodosian Code: Studies in the Imperial Law of Late Antiquity*, Duckworth, London

Hardy, E.G. (1889) *C.Plinii Caecilii Secundi Epistulae ad Traianum*, Oxford University Press

—— (1912) *Roman Laws and Charters*, Oxford University Press

Honoré, A.M. (1962) *Gaius*, Oxford University Press

—— (1965) 12 *RIDA*, 301–23, 'The *fragmentum Dositheanum*'

—— (1975) 65 *JRS*, 107–23, 'Some constitutions composed by Justinian'

—— (1978) *Tribonian*, Duckworth, London

—— (1979) 69 *JRS*, 51–64, 'Imperial rescripts AD 193–305; authorship and authenticity'

—— (1986) 103 *SZ*, 133–222, 'The making of the Theodosian Code'

Hunt, A.S. & C.C.Edgar (1932) *Select Papyri*, Loeb, London

Huschke, see *Iurisprudentia*

Jolowicz, H.F. & B.Nicholas (1972, 3rd edn) *Historical Introduction to the Study of Roman Law*, Cambridge University Press [= Jolowicz]

Jones, A.H.M. (1949) 39 *JRS*, 38–55, 'The Roman civil service (clerical and sub-clerical grades)'

—— (1950) 40 *JRS*, 22–9, The *aerarium* and the *fiscus*'

—— (1960) *Studies in Roman Government and Law*, Basil Blackwell, Oxford

—— (1964) *The Later Roman Empire 284–602*, Basil Blackwell, Oxford

—— (1972) *The Criminal Courts of the Roman Republic and Principate*, Basil Blackwell, Oxford

Kantorowicz, H. (1909–10) 30–1 *SZ*, 183–271 & 14-88, 'Über die Entstehung der Digestenvulgata'

Kaser, M. (1966) *Das römische Zivilprozessrecht*, Beck, Munich

—— (1967) 2 *IJ*, 129–43, 'The changing face of Roman jurisdiction'

—— (1971–4, 2nd edn) *Das römische Privatrecht*, Beck, Munich

—— (1978) 95 *SZ*, 15–92, 'Zum römischer Grabrecht'

—— (1984, tr. R.Dannenbring, 4th edn) *Roman Private Law*, Pretoria

Kelly, J.M. (1966a) *Roman Litigation*, Oxford University Press

—— (1966b) 1ns *IJ*, 341–55, 'The growth pattern of the praetor's edict'

—— (1976) *Studies in the Civil Judicature of the Roman Republic*, Oxford University Press

Keppie, L. (1991) *Understanding Roman Inscriptions*, London

Krüger, P. (1922) 43 *SZ*, 560–3, 'Neue juristische Funde aus Ägypten'

Kunkel, W. (1962) *Untersuchungen zur Entwicklung des römischen Kriminalverfahrens in vorsullanischen Zeit*, Munich

—— (1966, 2nd edn) *An Introduction to Roman Legal and Constitutional History*, tr. J.M.Kelly, Oxford University Press

—— (1967, 2nd edn) *Herkunft und soziale Stellung der römischen Juristen*, Graz/Vienna

—— (1967) & (1968) 84 & 85 *SZ*, 218–44 & 253–329, 'Die Funktion des Konsiliums in der magistratischen Strafjustiz und im Kaisergericht'

Lanciani, R. (1888) *Ancient Rome in the Light of Recent Discoveries*, London

—— (1897) *The Ruins and Excavations of Ancient Rome*, London

Lee, R.W. (1956, 3rd edn) *The Elements of Roman Law*, Sweet and Maxwell, London

Lenel, O. (1889 repr.1961) *Palingenesia Iuris Civilis*, Leipzig

—— (1927, 3rd edn repr.1956) *Das Edictum Perpetuum*, Leipzig

Levy, E. (1928) 48 *SZ*, 532–49(55), 'Neue Juristenfragmente aus Oxyrhynchos'

—— (1945) *Pauli Sententiae: a Palingenesia of the Opening Titles*, Cornell University Press

—— (1951) 55–6/14–15 *BIDR*, 222–58, 'Vulgarization of Roman law in the early Middle Ages as illustrated by successive versions of PS'

Lewis, A.D.E. & D.J.Ibbetson (eds) (1994) *The Roman Law Tradition*, Cambridge University Press

Liebs, D. (1964) *Hermogenians iuris Epitome*, Göttingen

—— (1987) *Die Jurisprudenz im spätantiken Italien (260–640 n.Chr.)*, Berlin

Lydus, Johannes, *On Powers [de magistratibus]*, ed. & tr. A.C.Bandy (Philadelphia 1983 – MemAPS vol. 149, 1982)

Maas, M. (1992) *John Lydus and the Roman Past*, Routledge, London

MacMullen, R. (1960) *Traditio*, repr. in *Changes in the Roman Empire* (Princeton University Press, 1990), 67–77, 'Roman bureaucratese'

—— (1980) 43 *P & P*, 3–16, 'Roman elite motivation'

—— (1986) 16 *Chiron*, 147–66, 'Judicial savagery in the Roman Empire'

—— (1988) *Corruption and the Decline of Rome*, Yale University Press

Mantovani, D. (1987) *Digesto e Masse Bluhmiane*, Milan

—— (1992) *Le formule nel processo privato*, Como

Marquardt, J. (1881–5) *Römische Staatsverwaltung*, Leipzig

Martino, F. de (1972–90, 2nd edn) *Storia della costituzione romana*, Naples

Matthews, J. (1993) 'The making of the text', 19–44 in J.Harries & I.Wood (eds) *The Theodosian Code: Studies in the Imperial Law of Late Antiquity*, Duckworth, London

Mattingly, H. (1960, 2nd edn) *Roman Coins*, London

Meyer, P.M. (1920) *Juristische Papyri. Erklärung von Urkunden zur Einführung in die juristische Papyruskunde*, Berlin

Milan Digest, see Bonfante

Millar, F. (1967) 57 *JRS*, 9–19, 'Emperors at work'

Mitteis, L. & U.Wilcken (1912) *Grundzüge und Chrestomathie der Papyruskunde*, Leipzig

Mommsen, T. (1887–8) *Römisches Staatsrecht*, Leipzig

Monro, C.H., tr. (1904–09) *Digest I–XV*, Cambridge University Press

Muirhead, J. (1880) *The Institutes of Gaius and Rules of Ulpian*, Edinburgh

Nelson, H.L.W. (1981) *Überlieferung, Aufbau und Stil von Gai Institutiones*, Leiden

Nicholas, B. (1962) *An Introduction to Roman Law*, Oxford University Press

Nicolet, C. (1958) 36 *RHD*, 260–75, 'Le sénat et les amendements aux lois à la fin de la République'

—— (1994) CAH IX², 599–643, ch. 16: 'Economy and society, 133–43 BC'

Nippel, W. (1995) *Public Order in Ancient Rome*, Cambridge University Press

Nörr, D. (1972) 89 *SZ*, 18–93, 'Spruchregel und Generalisierung'

—— (1981) 98 *SZ*, 1–46, 'Zur Reskriptenpraxis in der hohen Prinzipatzeit'

Pailler, J.M. (1988) *Bacchanalia: la repression de 186 av. J.C. à Rome et en Italie*, Rome

Palmer, R.E.A. (1980) 'Customs on market goods imported into the City of Rome', 217–33 in J.H.D'Arms & E.C.Kopff (eds) *The Seaborne Commerce of Ancient Rome*, American Academy, Rome

Pauly-Wissowa, *Realencyclopädie der klassischen Altertumswissenschaft*, ed. G.Wissowa, W.Kroll et al. (1893–) [= PW/RE]

Pennsylvania Digest, see Watson

Pharr, C. (tr.) (1952) *The Theodosian Code*, University of Texas, Austin

Premerstein, A.von (1900) *PW 4*, 220–2, '*A cognitionibus*'

Purcell, N. (1983) 51 *PBSR*, 125–73, 'The *apparitores*'

Raber, F. (1965) *PW Supp. 10*, 231–41, 'Fragmenta iuris Vaticana'

Robertis, F. M.de (1982) *ANRW* II 14, 791–815, '*Lis fullonum*: CIL VI 266'

Robinson, O.F. (1968) 15 *RIDA*, 389–98, 'Private prisons'

—— (1975) 10 *IJ*, 175–86, 'The Roman law of burials and burial grounds'

—— (1981) 98 *SZ*, 213–54, 'Slaves and the criminal law'

—— (1985) *St. Moschella – 8 Ann.Perugia*, 527–60, 'Women and the criminal law'

—— (1987) *JR*, 143–62, 'The status of women in Roman private law'

—— (1990–2) 25–7 *IJ*, 269–92, 'The repression of Christians in the pre-Decian period: a legal problem still'

—— (1991–2) 33–4 *BIDR*, 89–104, 'Some thoughts on Justinian's summary of Roman criminal law'

—— (1992, revised paperback 1994) *Ancient Rome: city planning and administration*, Routledge, London

—— (1995) *Criminal Law at Rome*, Duckworth, London

—— (1996) 17 *JLH*, 130–43, 'The role of the Senate in Roman criminal law during the Principate'

Robinson, O.F., T.D.Fergus & W.M.Gordon (1994, 2nd edn, amended from 1992 edn) *An Introduction to European Legal History*, Butterworth, London [= ELH]

Rodger, A. (1991) 81 *JRS*, 74–90, 'The *lex Irnitana* and procedure in the civil courts'

Rotondi, G. (1912 repr.1966) *Leges publicae populi romani*, Milan

Ruggiero, E.de (1886–) *Dizionario epigrafico di antichità romana*, Rome

Schiller, A.A. (1954) see *Apokrimata*

—— (1971) *Atti II della Società Italiana per la Storia di Diritto*, Florence, vol. II, 717–27, 'La critica del testo: Vindication of a repudiated text'

—— (1978) *Roman Law: Mechanisms of Development*, Mouton

Schott, C. (1979) 13 *Frühmittelaltliche Studien*, 29–55, 'Der Stand der Leges-Forschung'

Schulz, F. (1926) *Die Epitome Ulpiani des Codex Vaticanus Reginae 1128*, Bonn

—— (1936) *Principles of Roman Law*, Oxford University Press

—— (1953, original edn 1946) *History of Roman Legal Science*, Oxford University Press

Scott, S.P. (tr.) (1932) *The Civil Law*, Cincinnati

Seeck, see *Notitia Dignitatum*

Seckel-Kübler = *Iurisprudentia*

Selb, W. (1984) *Gedächtnisschrift für W.Kunkel*, 391–448, 'Vom geschichtlichen Wandel der Aufgabe des *iudex* in der *legis actio*', Frankfurt am Main

—— (1990) *Sententiae Syriacae*, Vienna

Serrao, F. (1954) *La iurisdictio del pretore peregrino*, Milan

—— (1956) *Il frammento Leidense di Paolo*, Milan

Sherwin-White, A.N. (1966) *The Letters of Pliny*, Oxford University Press

Simshaüser, W. (1990) 107 *SZ*, 543–61, review article on the *lex Irnitana* publications

Sirks, B. (1993) 'The Sources of the Code', 45–67 in J.Harries & I.Wood (eds) *The Theodosian Code: Studies in the Imperial Law of Late Antiquity*, Duckworth, London

Smith, J.A. Clarence (1970) 14 *AmJLH*, 157–83 & 247–75, 'Bartolo and the conflict of laws'

Stein, P. (1966) *Regulae Iuris*, Aberdeen

Studia Gaiana IV (1956), see Archi

Talbert, R.J.A. (1984) *The Senate of Imperial Rome*, Princeton University Press

—— (1985) *Atlas of Classical History*, Routledge, London

Taubenschlag, R. (1955, 2nd edn) *The Law of Greco-Roman Egypt in the light of the Papyri*, Warsaw

Teitler, H.C. (1985) *Notarii and Exceptores*, Gieben, Amsterdam

Tellegen-Couperus, O.E. (1993) *A Short History of Roman Law*, Routledge, London

Thomas, J.A.C. (1963) 31 *TR*, 39–53, 'Custom and Roman law'

—— (1975) *The Institutions of Justinian*, Cape Town

—— (1976) *Textbook of Roman Law*, Amsterdam/New York

Thompson, E.A. (1947) *The Historical Works of Ammianus Marcellinus*, Cambridge University Press

Tomulescu, C.St. (1971) 18 *RIDA*, 691–710, 'Le droit romain dans les triptyques de Transylvanie'

Tortorici, E. (1991) *Argiletum: commercio, speculazione edilizia e lotta politica*, Rome

Turpin, W. (1991) 81 *JRS*, 101–18, 'Imperial subscriptions and the administration of justice'

Vessey, M. (1993) 'The origins of the *Collectio Sirmondiana*', 178–99, in J.Harries & I.Wood (eds) *The Theodosian Code: Studies in the Imperial Law of Late Antiquity*, Duckworth, London

Visscher, F. de (1963) *Le droit des tombeaux romains*, Milan

Vismara, G. (1967) *Edictum Theodorici*, IRMAE, Milan

Warmington, E.H. (1938, revised 1967) *Remains of Old Latin*, vol. ii, Loeb, London

Watson, A. (1968) 58 *JRS*, 105–19, 'The development of the Praetor's Edict'

—— (1970) *The Law of the Ancient Romans*, Southern Methodist University Press, Dallas

—— (1972a) 62 *JRS*, 100–5, 'Roman private law and the *leges regiae*'

—— (1972b) *Israel LR*, 14–24, 'Illogicality and Roman law'

—— (1973) 41 *TR*, 19–34, 'Private law in the rescripts of Carus, Carinus, and Numerianus'

—— (1974a) *Law Making in the Roman Republic*, Oxford University Press

—— (1974b) 48 *Tul.LR*, 1122–8, 'The rescripts of the Emperor Probus (272–182 AD)'

—— (1976) 92 *LQR*, 79–84, 'Legal transplants and law reform'

—— (1985) ed. translation of the *Digest*, University of Pennsylvania Press

—— (1987) 29 *BIDR*, 105–18, 'Slavery and the development of Roman private law'

—— (1991) *Roman Law and Comparative Law*, University of Georgia Press

—— (1992) *The State, Law and Religion: Pagan Rome*, University of Georgia Press

—— (1994) 62 *TR*, 113–25, '*Prolegomena* to establishing pre-Justinianic texts'

—— (1995) *The Spirit of Roman Law*, University of Georgia Press

Weaver, P.R.C. (1972) *Familia Caesaris*, Cambridge University Press

Wenger, L. (1953) *Die Quellen des römischen Rechts*, Holzhausen, Vienna

Westermann, W.L. (1954) see *Apokrimata*

Willems, P. (1885) *Le sénat de la république romaine*, Louvain

Williams, W. (1974) 64 *JRS*, 86–103, 'The *libellus* procedure and the Severan papyri'

—— (1976) 66 *JRS*, 67–83, 'Individuality in the imperial constitutions'

—— (1990) *Pliny the Younger: Correspondence with Trajan from Bithynia*, Aris & Philips, Warminster

Wiseman, T.P. (1994) CAH IX², 327–67, ch. 9: 'The Senate and the *populares*, 69–60 BC'

Wolf, J.G. & J.A.Crook (1989) *Rechtsurkunden in Vulgarlatein*, Heidelberg

Wolff, H.-J. (1949) *Scritti Ferrini* IV, 64–90, 'Ulpian XVII *ad edictum* in *Collatio* and Digest and the problem of post-classical editions of classical works'

—— (1951) *Roman Law: an historical introduction*, University of Oklahoma Press

Index of Sources

Epigraphic Sources

FIRA

Tacitus

Varro

General Index